TRIATHLON SWIMMING FOUNDATIONS

A Straightforward System for Making Beginner Triathletes Comfortable and Confident in the Water

"TRIATHLON TAREN" GESELL

ISBN: 978-1-0874-2212-1

CONTENTS

CHAPTER 1

C'MON IN, THE WATER'S WARM

INTRO

"I'd love to do triathlon, but I'd never be able to do the swim."

"I just need to get through the swim and get to my bike. Then, I'll be fine."

"When I took up triathlon, I thought if I could learn to swim, I could do this sport. Twenty years later, I'm still thinking if I could learn to swim, I could do this sport."

Those comments (or others just like them) have been said by countless triathletes who didn't swim much as kids. In my experience, only one of every 20 (or heck, every 50) triathletes has a solid swim background. Yet, we find ourselves competing in a sport that starts with an organized mosh pit in the water for upwards of 2.4 miles surrounded by a couple thousand of our closest friends.

If any of the above sounds like something you've said to yourself, I want this book to bring you hope. Of all three disciplines in triathlon, swimming might be the easiest in which to make improvements. While cycling improvement takes an enormous amount of time in the saddle and running is very dependent on our natural biomechanics and susceptibility to injury, triathletes can easily become top-10-percent-of-the-field swimmers with just three one-hour swims per week. So, why do triathletes continue to struggle in the water? There are a number of reasons.

Water is such a foreign environment that we're all essentially newborns in Speedos; we have to learn how to swim the same way we learned to walk. Our parents didn't just stand us up and say, "Figure it out, kid." They allowed us to learn the skills we would need: first sitting up, then becoming aware of our legs, pulling ourselves up on furniture, and walking with help, before eventually walking on our own. So, in the same vein, we can't expect to jump in the water and do a great swim workout without learning proper swim technique from the start.

I'm going to introduce you to a typical age-group triathlete who might sound familiar. This athlete is taking up triathlon in his mid-thirties. He wants to get healthier and figures triathlon would be a cool bucket-list thing to do. He has played some competitive sports in the past but he let himself get out of shape while working his office job. Other than getting through don't drown levels 1–6 as a kid, he doesn't have much of a swim background. He tries to swim two or three times a week and he's determined to figure out the triathlon swim.

When this athlete swam for the very first time after deciding to tackle his first triathlon, he jumped into the pool thinking, "I swam a little when I was a kid. Let's just dust off the cobwebs." Over the following hour, he only managed to swim 14 total laps (350 yards) and he had to stop in the middle of the pool a dozen times. He needed breaks after every single lap, he choked on the water, and he lost his breath constantly. When he finally got to work after swimming, he was blowing chlorine out of his nose for hours.

Does this bring back traumatic memories from when you first got back in the pool? If so, you're not alone! This is a rite of passage almost every adult triathlete goes through.

Swimming is one of the most unnatural movements humans could possibly do. We evolved to walk around all day long, breathing oxygen. We use our eyes to see where we're going, we hold ourselves upright, and we move forward with our legs. Swimming, on the other hand, happens under water with no oxygen. We can't really see where we're going (and sometimes we can't even see our hands in front of our faces in open water), we're in a horizontal prone position, and we have to create most of our forward movement with our arms instead of our legs.

See? It's among the most unnatural things a human could do! And don't even get me started about the deep-water sea monsters I'm still convinced are just waiting for the right race to take me out.

Let's go back to that typical age-group triathlete from a few paragraphs ago. After a couple years of struggling to swim on his own, he decided to take triathlon seriously so he joined a masters swim group and started getting occasional one-on-one swim instruction from a local coach. Great idea, right? Not so fast.

Let's think about how that person became a swim coach. More often than not, coaches become coaches because they were elite swimmers themselves in the past but usually not triathlon swimmers. Because of that, they coach triathlon swimmers the same way they were coached as young swimmers themselves. Unfortunately, this lack of knowledge of the specifics of triathlon swimming can lead to well-meaning but inappropriate instruction.

When elite swimmers grow up training for speed, they generally have genetically gifted bodies and training schedules that we age-group triathletes can only dream of. For example:

- Elite swimmers have the body flexibility of Gumby. We age-group triathletes typically have a lifetime of desk work in our now-stiff upper bodies and a load of running in our legs which decreases our ankle flexibility. We simply can't move the same way elite swimmers do.

- Elite swimmers often train for events where 90 percent of their races last three minutes or less; the swim portion of triathlons are anywhere from 10 minutes to two hours. Do you think our swims might require a different method of training?

- Elite swimmers get to empty the tank in their swim race, hang out on the pool wall for a minute or two, and then go sit in a hot tub for half an hour. Meanwhile, triathletes swim like crazy for a long distance in open water then proceed to cycle and run for up to 15 more hours.

- Elite swimmers have only one sport to train for so they can train more than 10 times a week, amassing up to seventy thousand yards. Do any of you have time for that?

- Elite swimmers train and race in perfect, controlled conditions. Pools have big lane ropes to knock down any "waves," a nice black line on the bottom of the pool to follow, flags overhead to tell swimmers how far the wall is, and gutters to make the pool as calm as possible. Contrast that with the blind chaos we endure in the open water (not to mention the unpredictable conditions) and you almost start envying those elite swimmers.

Do you see how not all swimming is the same? So, what happens when former elite/speed swimmers teach age-group triathletes how to swim? The coaches often try to fit a square peg into a round hole. They instruct age-group triathletes to do things only elite swimmers are typically capable of. In many cases, this does more harm than good.

Take kicking, the bane of most age-group triathletes' existence. Elite swimmers cover tens of thousands of yards each week, working on their kick, usually with their hands clasped on the front of a kickboard and their heads out of the water. This approach causes a problem for age-group triathletes. First, we don't have enough back flexibility or body awareness to stick our heads out of the water while still keeping our feet at the surface of the water. As such, traditional kick drills actually encourage age-group swimmers to drop their legs in the water—if the head goes up, the legs go down like a seesaw in the water. This exacerbates one of the top problems age-group triathletes have: sinking legs.

Beyond making the sinking legs worse, traditional mindless meters of kicking don't have a big return on investment for triathletes. Even elite swimmers only get a maximum of 10-15 percent of their forward propulsion from kicking[1], while we age-group swimmers only get between 0 and 5 percent. (In fact, some even have "negative propulsion." Have you ever seen someone who kicked and moved backward? It's a thing!) So even if we did improve our kick by double, it might only amount to a slight improvement in total propulsion.

---

[1] https://www.arenawaterinstinct.com/en_uk/community/training-technique/science-swimming-mysteries-freestyle-leg-kick/

I'm going to keep ranting about kicking for a moment but bear with me because this is a big topic for triathletes.

The legs are huge muscle groups and require a ton of oxygen. Turning them over at a high rate shoots the heart rate up dramatically, strips the body of oxygen, increases the burning lactic acid feeling, and even causes the panic many new age-group triathletes report as soon as they start swimming even a little bit hard. Elite swimmers can tough out these issues for the short duration of their races, but triathletes need to conserve as much energy as possible so we can be fresh for the bike and the run.

Finally, elite swimmers put in tens of thousands of yards every week to improve their kick just slightly. Age-group triathletes swim far less, and we don't have the luxury of time to dedicate solely to kicking.

And this problem with former elite swimmers-turned coaches handing down unrealistic swim instruction to age-group triathletes isn't limited to kicking. Drills like side kicking, doing hypoxic breathing sets, spending too much time on flip turns, and training an early vertical forearm or a high elbow recovery are just a few of the "elite swimming family heirlooms" that realistically don't need to be prescribed for triathlon swimmers.

Don't get me wrong, I have the utmost respect for elite swimmers and swim coaches but I've seen it time and time again when their advice just isn't triathlon-swim appropriate because they've never done a triathlon themselves, and because age-groupers aren't physiologically the same as elite swimmers.

Now, let's turn our attention to the triathlon media for a second. It's no secret swimming is the discipline most triathletes struggle with. Writers, bloggers, podcasters, and coaches know it gets views so they flood triathletes with an enormous amount of swim content, which can be confusing.

I'm no saint here: I'll admit, I add to the problem. Take a look at a screenshot of the ten most popular videos of all time on my YouTube channel. Half of the videos are about swim instruction. At the time of writing, these five videos alone amounted to more than 6 percent of my all-time views. (And I had posted around 900 videos at the time.)

It's time to meet back up with that typical age-grouper we talked about earlier. After struggling through races for two years while training on his own, then joining a masters swim group and continuing to struggle mightily through swim workouts, he decides to head to the internet to learn as much as he can about swimming.

Quickly, he finds answers. Just as quickly, he realizes a lot of the information is conflicting. One article says swimmers should use a six-beat kick, while sexy online videos show an effortless-looking two-beat kick. Another series of videos shows elite open-water swimmers with 80–100 arm strokes per minute while an Instagram influencer shows video after video of how easy swimming can be at a yawn-worthy 30 strokes per minute. Then there are some coaches saying not to worry about the swim because it's such a small portion of the race that improving your swim won't have much of an effect on your overall performance.

This person tries one drill that promises to improve his sinking legs and he actually gets pretty good at it. During the drill, his legs float up to the surface but when he starts swimming normally, his legs drag down just like before. He then tries an easy-looking stroke paired with a two-beat kick he's seen on YouTube. Sure enough, it feels way easier in the pool for a 25-yard length but he can't hold that form in open water. (And he can't go any faster than a warm-up pace.)

After a few years in triathlon, our age-group athlete is just as frustrated with swimming as he was on his first day. It's not his fault; he's done everything he thinks he should do. He's hired coaches, joined clubs, done organized group workouts, and bought all kinds of gear but he still can't get comfortable in the water. He's less frightened of race day but even with all the effort he's put in, he's barely any faster.

The good news is this, athlete: it's not you, it's swimming! All those experiences our friend went through are the challenges most triathletes encounter when they try to work on their swimming. These problems are as much a part of swimming as sore bums are to cycling. But like I said before, hope is not lost! There's plenty we can do.

If you've watched my YouTube channel, this athlete might sound familiar to you. The athlete is actually me! And, that experience is exactly what I went through during my first few years in triathlon. I struggled to breathe in the water for years. I battled legs so "sinky" that during some drills, they actually bounced off the bottom of the pool. I was afraid of the water for my entire adolescence and often had a heart rate so high at the start of triathlons that my peak heart rate for the entire race was during the first couple minutes after the gun went off.

Fortunately, there came a point where I realized I had to dismantle my swim (the entire swimming process, actually) and start right from square one, re-learning how to swim.

As of today, I've swum a nonstop open-water marathon swim of 27 kilometers (16.8 miles) over seven hours, and a record-setting nonstop 37-kilometer (23 mile), nine-hour swim that you can see on YouTube. Tune into my Instagram feed and you'll see, each week, I complete a four to five thousand-yard swim, averaging 1:30 per 100 yards (and getting faster each month.) In race after race, I come out of the water among the top 10 percent of the field. I get on the bike feeling fresh, not having taxed myself on the swim whatsoever.

Believe it or not, the swim has become one of the most enjoyable aspects of triathlon for me. I look forward to getting to the start line of a race because I'm calm, I can rely on my hundreds of great training sessions in the pool, and I know I've got a leg up on the struggling swimmers all around me.

That dismantling process I went through, combined with the lessons I've gained from working with some of the best triathlon-specific swim coaches in the world, is what has resulted in the Trainiac Swimming System you're about to learn in this booklet.

A couple final notes. First, this book is not in competition with your local swim coaches, masters swim groups, or triathlon clubs. Rather, this book is a primer, a guide to help prepare you if you decide to join those swim groups so you don't hop into a workout like a newborn and have a bad experience. So instead of looking at this book as an alternative to traditional swim instruction, view it as filling an unserved need and taking people from not swimming at all to being comfortable enough in the water to join any swim group or race they want to enter.

Last thing, this book works in conjunction with the free drill videos that you can find at triathlontaren.com/swimfoundations. By entering your email address there, you'll get the video demonstrations and explanations to execute the drills laid out in this book. While I've described the drills you need to perform, there are nuances for each drill with regards to things you should focus on, common things triathletes get wrong when performing the drills, specific hand placement, and so on. Even if you think you understand what I've written in this book, please go to triathlontaren.com/swimfoundations to make sure you're performing the drills perfectly and not wasting time doing things incorrectly.

THE JOURNEY TO THE FRONT SWIM PACK

When I was a kid, I was scared of the water—so scared, I'd rush to the ladder as quickly as possible after every cannonball because I was convinced there was a shark in our backyard pool. True story. To this day, I still have moments during open water swims when I wonder if a sea monster is waiting to strike.

That story I told you about swimming just 14 lengths over the course of an hour and having to take breaks after every length was true. All of those stories are true. I suffered nearly every possible swim problem triathletes encounter when they start swimming:

- I felt out of breath and my body ached from (what I thought was) a lack of oxygen.
- My legs sank REALLY low in the water.
- I was jittery with nerves before every single race.

- I had to take breaks mid-swim to catch my breath during races.
- My watch GPS tracker showed I consistently swam off course in every race, extending my swim by 10-20 percent.
- I'd spend the first 10-15 minutes of the bike recovering from the trauma of the swim.

As I mentioned at the end of the last chapter, I now have zero—and I mean ZERO—problems with swimming! In fact, now I love it. But let's get something straight: I'm still not an elite swimmer. I'm just an age-group triathlete who has become totally confident in the water. The only difference between you and me is, I've gone through a process of trial and error, research, hard lessons, and exposure to the best swim coaches in the world. As a result, I've gotten over my early struggles.

And that's exactly what I'm going to share with you: the system and training I've used to get myself to this point. This system can be used by anyone, regardless of swim background, physical abilities, or time allotments for swimming.

That said, improving my swimming wasn't a quick process for me and I'm not going to tell you this booklet will be the magic bullet for you either. What I will tell you is that I'm taking my 10 years of research and work with the top swim coaches in the field and giving you the simple and easy information you need to change your experience in the water.

As I've worked with more and more athletes, this system has evolved and been simplified into the following three parts that will guide you toward becoming the strong swimmer you want to be:

1.   Breathe Like a Dolphin

2.   Float Like a Log

3.   Race Like an Arrow

I'll elaborate on each of these over the course of the book. What you need to know right now is, by focusing on just these three things, you won't need 10 years to make improvements like I did. In only a few weeks, you'll start to notice improvements. In a few months, you'll feel like a completely different swimmer.

After a swim analysis and just four weeks of doing our Team Trainiac-prescribed workouts, which are based on the same principles as in this book, one Trainiac wrote:

I wanted to let you know that the swim workouts in the platform have had huge benefits in a short amount of time. I went to the Masters swim for the first time in a month and not only felt great working at a higher effort level, but I lead the lane the whole time and came out with an average eight seconds faster per 100!

This system has been developed with a lot of other influences, both good and bad. I've taken the bad advice and implemented wrong strategies so you don't have to. That's why I can confidently tell you which things to embrace and what not to waste your time on.

As of writing this book, we've had almost 15,000 athletes go through our basic "learn to swim" program. We've received hundreds of messages from people saying our program has stopped them from hyperventilating, made them finally enjoy swimming, and they're getting faster all the time.

That said, I can write all the swim workouts I want, perform swim analysis after swim analysis, and prescribe drill after drill, but if the athletes don't do the work, they won't make improvements.

I can lead a triathlete to water but I can't make them work.

Improvement will require effort on your part, and here's what's required:

- ➢ Swim two to four times per week, every week, for the prescribed durations indicated in this system.
- ➢ Perform the drills and swimming as prescribed, no substitutions or omissions.
- ➢ Swim with purpose. DO NOT swim mindlessly without paying attention to your form, effort levels, or the workout structure.

If you can't commit to these requirements, this swim system isn't for you because this isn't a "get fast quick" scheme. We require dedication and focus. If you come to the pool deck with that, I'll give you a system that will transform your swimming and get you closer to that front pack.

Let's get into it, Trainiacs!

BEFORE YOU DIVE IN

Before getting into the actual swim instruction, we need to talk about what swimming is and what swimming isn't. These are the critical swimming DOS and the critical swimming DON'TS.

The key to swimming well is not simply spending tons of time in the water. That concept can be confusing to some triathletes because it's very different than cycling or running where the more you work, the better you get. It's actually possible that if you swim too much while you have bad technique, you'll engrain those incorrect muscle patterns into your body. Swimming also isn't about building a big aerobic engine like in running; look at any masters swim group and you'll see people who appear to be pretty out of shape, right alongside 60-plus-year-old swimmers, leading in the fastest lanes. None of these lane-one swimmers are aerobic machines. They swim well because of technique.

Swimming well really is about technique, plain and simple—not lung capacity, muscle endurance, flexibility, or core strength, just some basic and easy-to-perform principles of technique. Of course, at the elite levels of speed swimming, those factors certainly do make a big difference but those swimmers are looking to be in the top 1 percent of the top 1 percent in the world. At the triathlon age-group level, the vast majority of the swimmers you're competing against are struggling too. All we need is an easy-to-learn system to get you comfortable and capable in the water.

We also need a system that's uniquely designed for the open-water needs of a triathlete. I recently met a person whose friend was an elite-level swimmer who decided to enter a triathlon and concentrate only on the bike and the run because she thought she had the swim nailed down. This athlete got into the water on race day and ended up having to be pulled out of the water by kayaks because the open-water swim—in a wetsuit, with sighting requirements, and with people around her—was so different from the pool swimming she was used to that it may as well have been a new sport.

This would have been very easy to prevent because at this level of triathlon swimming, the capabilities we need to develop are based on the three very easy-to-learn core principles we mentioned in the last chapter:

1. Breathe Like a Dolphin: You need to be able to breathe without stress.

2. Float Like a Log: You need to be at the surface of the water without your legs sinking.

3. Race Like an Arrow: You need to swim straight without having your legs sway side to side, and without swimming off course.

BREATHE LIKE A DOLPHIN

Picture a dolphin surfacing on the water to grab air. It's subtle, effortless, and quick. That's what we're aiming for: subtle, effortless, and quick. In other words, easy.

Through our breathing drill progression, you'll develop the instant reflex to breathe properly during all of your swimming, no matter how hard you're racing. You won't feel out of breath, your body won't burn, and all panicked feelings will go away.

Correct swim breathing technique: one goggle lens in water, head does not lift, small breath grabbed from the bow created by the head.

FLOAT LIKE A LOG

Think about pushing a log across the surface of the water; it moves easily and without a lot of effort. Now picture pushing a tree branch with a bunch of smaller branches going in different directions across the water. It's a total pain and the branch feels like it weighs hundreds of pounds.

The differences between the log and the tree branch are that the log is stiff and straight with almost no drag, while the branch twists and turns, creating drag everywhere. We want to swim like the log: firm, straight, and without drag. This will make you faster and keep your legs from sinking below the surface. Our floating drill progression will teach you how to do all of this.

Correct floating technique: back of head, butt, and heels at the surface of the water.

RACE LIKE AN ARROW

Let's say a triathlete builds a nice stiff body and is at the surface of the water like the log but her feet sway side-to-side as she moves across the pool. The swaying creates drag, which slows her down.

Or let's say that triathlete is even one step better: she's nice and firm in the water, like the log, AND she swims with a straight body line BUT she doesn't know how to sight and swims slightly off course in each race she does. This athlete may be swimming fast but is ultimately swimming a longer distance than other athletes, effectively making her time slower.

With our open-water swim drills, we'll have you swimming with good technique and proper sighting so you swim the shortest distance possible in every race.

By accomplishing these three simple principles, you'll be comfortable and capable, putting you ahead of likely 70-80 percent of the field at the start line of every race you enter.

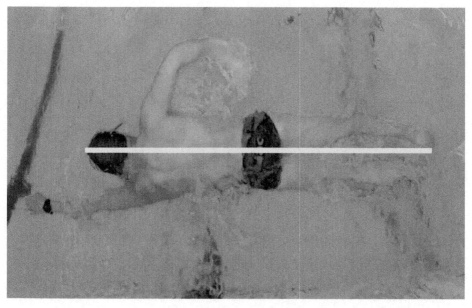

Race Like an Arrow technique: middle of head, lower back, and feet all in line, pointing dead straight.

Comfort and **capacity** are words I've chosen very intentionally. I didn't choose expertise, I didn't choose proficiency, and I didn't even choose skill. To be close to the front swim pack in a lot of races, all you really need is to be comfortable and capable. Those two attributes are easy to build with the right system, done consistently and patiently, over time.

The system in this book isn't going to require you to swim huge amounts. To improve in the swim, we don't need to swim 14 times a week like elite swimmers. We just need to do the right things more often.

Jimmy Seear, co-founder of the bike company Ventum, was a 10-time podium finisher on the ITU triathlon circuit and managed one first-place finish in international ITU racing. At this level of racing, being an elite swimmer is the price of admission; if these athletes can't swim in the front pack, they won't make the front bike pack and they're basically out of the race before they get out of T1. I was once at Jimmy's house in Boulder, working on my Ventum bike, and he told me how his former ITU competitors were consistently swimming 50,000 yards or more each week while he was swimming just 25,000 yards in an average week. He said he looked at his competitors' swim workouts and realized they were just swimming for the sake of swimming. Sure, they had a coach who provided them with workouts and a total season plan but they weren't working on the right things, the things that allowed Jimmy to get away with swimming half as much as his competitors were.

Even at ITU triathlon levels, swimming doesn't have to be about piling on the yards. As Jimmy proved, it can still be about the right system.

Now, to be clear, this doesn't mean you barely need to swim. In fact, most of you reading this will need to swim more often than you are right now. Swimming twice a week is okay, and beginners will make some progress with this amount of swimming. Three swims a week is a good sweet spot for a lot of athletes to see progress. But four sessions a week is where you need to be to see huge gains if you're working on the right things. However, with anything beyond four swims a week, diminishing returns start to creep in and it's not worth it for the average age-grouper.

"Why focus on the swim at all when it's such a small portion of the overall race?" some of you might ask. Matt Dixon, head coach of Purple Patch Fitness, has been called the best triathlon coach in the world by many highly respected triathlon coaches and athletes. Matt has taken a large number of athletes with zero triathlon background (albeit most of them do have elite sports backgrounds) and turned them into world-class, professional triathletes: Jesse Thomas, Sarah Piampiano, Laura Siddall, and most recently Chelsea Sodoro. Matt once said he has never seen an athlete who put an increased focus on swimming do anything besides become an overall better triathlete.

One thing to keep in mind, though, is that once you develop a solid capacity in the water, swimming will have a smaller and smaller effect on your overall triathlon performance. In reviewing massive data sets of hundreds of thousands of 70.3 and IRONMAN finish times, I found that fast bike times were very strongly correlated with fast overall times, run times were just slightly less correlated with overall triathlon times, and swim times were significantly less correlated with overall triathlon finish times. So pounding out millions of yards of swimming won't necessarily make you a better triathlete alone but you need to have enough capability in the water that you don't get on the bike totally spent for the rest of the race. Beyond that, swimming does offer ancillary benefits to triathlon that aren't just a direct "fast swim time."

There are several reasons improving your swim can improve your overall triathlon performance, primarily that swimming has an enormously beneficial effect on both biking and running. The same can't always be said about the opposite.

While running is compressive and biking scrunches us up, swimming lengthens out the body, making athletes carry themselves more upright and taller. This helps with overall posture and body structure for the run and the bike.

Running at super-high intensities on the track to build our top end of aerobic fitness is VERY high impact, thus risky, and can really only be done once per week. Swimming is low risk and you can red-line it several days a week without risk of injury, meaning you can work on building your top end of fitness more often.

Swimming is also restorative. Running breaks us down, beats us up, and creates knots and niggles. Biking in the aero position makes our chests tight and degrades our posture, slowly putting us into a more hunched position. The right recovery swim workouts help fix those issues so we can get back to training hard across all three disciplines.

We need to swim, we need to swim somewhat frequently, and we need to focus on the right things when we swim. So, what are the really big-picture things you should and should not focus on to make progress in swimming?

CRITICAL SWIMMING DOS

1. DO swim at least twice a week, every week.

2. DO swim longer than most triathletes swim during at least one workout per week.

3. DO swim with a purpose to every single part of every single swim workout (no mindless laps).

4. DO get an in-water swim video analysis (not just an on-deck analysis) done by a triathlon-specific swim instructor twice per year.

5. DO practice your open-water skills in the pool.

6. DO gain an understanding of the proper use of all swim toys.

7. DO take a step back every so often to focus on technique basics.

8. DO think critically about anything you hear about swimming before implementing it into your training.

CRITICAL SWIMMING DON'TS

1. DON'T buy into the belief that swimming is only a small portion of the race so you don't need to worry about it.

2. DON'T believe that just swimming regularly, without thought to the structure of workouts and season progression, will improve your swim.

3. DON'T perform drills or any part of a workout without an understanding by you or your instructor as to why this drill is prescribed for age-group triathletes.

4. DON'T use swim toys blindly.

5. DON'T EVER call yourself a crappy swimmer! You're simply a developing triathlete.

CHAPTER 2

BREATHE LIKE A DOLPHIN

BREATHING INTRO

When I hopped in the pool for my first-ever triathlon training swim (remember my "typical triathlete" story from the introduction), I did some math. I knew I could hold my breath for a minute on land yet I needed 10-15 breaths in the 45 seconds it took me to cross the pool one time. Why was I out of breath? And why did I need to take a break for a minute at the wall after every single lap?

When we were babies and went from sitting on the floor to walking, it was a completely foreign thing. We learned over the course of many weeks and gradually became more comfortable with the necessary balance, movement patterns, and muscle control. Soon enough, we were running to the nearest baseboard heater to stick a plastic ruler in it and force a mass building evacuation (or at least I did).

When we start swimming, it's not much different. We didn't go from crawling on the floor to putting rulers in baseboard heaters in a second, so we can't expect to pick up breathing while swimming in a second either. When triathletes first start swimming and don't spend any time doing drills to train their brain to tell their lungs to breathe while in the water, it's setting them up to feel short of breath, have a full-body burning sensation, and potentially hyperventilate or panic.

People normally take 12–20 breaths per minute at rest. During intense exercise, it's 40-50 breaths. Most new triathletes have a stroke count in the range of 40–60 and will breathe every second or third stroke. So they're breathing only 13–30 times per minute while exerting themselves.

Making this worse is that it's a natural reflex for triathletes to hold their breath when they swim in order to keep oxygen in and water out. This leads to a buildup of carbon dioxide in the body which is the main signal to the brain that it's time to take more breaths.

It's the perfect storm of breathing problems:

- Triathletes are only taking in a quarter to half as many breaths as they actually need.
- They're in a foreign environment, creating an elevated heart rate and a fight-or-flight response in the body.

- CO_2 builds up in the body which leads the brain to scream, "I need to breathe!!!"

The result is panicking, stopping halfway down the length of the pool, or even stopping during a race in the ocean/lake/river and potentially being pulled out of the water by the safety kayaks.

This is exactly what I went through during that first triathlon training swim, and continued to struggle with literally for years. In fact, if you look at my Triathlon Taren YouTube channel, the most popular video I've ever done is called "Breathe Easier Swimming" with almost 200k views as of this writing. Shortly behind that are "Triathlon Swimming Tricks So You Don't Lose Your Breath", "Breathe Less If You're Out of Breath Triathlon Swimming", and "Panic Free Open Water Swimming."

Nearly everyone goes through this but fortunately, breathing while swimming will be one of the easiest things you learn to do. But it wasn't until I took a step back from swimming and started over from scratch that breathing became easy. Triathletes won't solve their breathing issues just by swimming more without purpose. That's why, if you genuinely want to get a handle on triathlon swimming, you need to stop what you're struggling with and take a step back so you can ultimately take many leaps forward.

BREATHING TECHNIQUE

The breathing technique and drills you're going to learn will require you to hit pause on what you're doing right now in the pool. It's going to feel like a step back but don't worry. This "step back" is temporary, perhaps lasting just a week or two. After going through this routine, you'll be able to breathe while swimming, without thinking about it, and it will never be a problem again.

When we start to address breathing during swimming, we have to accomplish a few things:

1. We need to keep CO_2 from building up in our lungs, causing us to feel out of breath.

2. We need to develop a new breathing pattern because we don't have the luxury of breathing whenever our bodies feel like it, which they do during exercise on land.

3. We need to supply our muscles with enough oxygen to fuel the efforts we're putting out.

These are the common faults that lead to swim breathing problems and other swim technique issues:

1. Holding the breath.

2. Craning the neck and lifting the head to breathe (We'll talk more about this in the section called "Float Like a Log.")

3. Taking too-big breaths.

4. Not breathing out constantly while the face is in the water.

5. Breathing less than once every two strokes.

What's the correct swim breathing technique?

1. Exhale the entire time your face is in the water.

2. Turn your head just slightly to breathe.

3. Take only a small sip of air each time you breathe.

4. Breathe every two strokes to give yourself as much air as possible.

Perform these four things and you'll breathe just fine throughout your entire triathlon career. But I know that's easier said than done. Think about when you've been really scared and your body tensed up. It probably wasn't so easy to breathe in a calm and controlled manner. When we find ourselves in a hard situation, the body begins the fight-or-flight response, tensing up, releasing adrenaline, and getting into a very "on edge" status. This isn't conducive to breathing while swimming.

When you start dedicating yourself to learning the basics of swimming, you'll have to retrain your body and brain completely; you'll have to train your body to perform a new breathing pattern and your brain to stay calm in the water.

The progression of swim drills we're about to share with you will accomplish both. You'll be able to breathe calmly (or quickly, when putting out increased effort), you won't panic in the water, and you'll never have to worry about your breathing holding you back in the water again.

BREATHING PROGRESSION

With all of our drills, we'll be building from one skill to the next in tiny increments. We'll give you all of the tools and guidelines to master a drill. Your job is to perform the work patiently until you've got a solid handle on it and then incorporate the next drill, improving one step at a time.

The sequence of how to perform these drills with regard to where they should be put in a workout, how many laps of them to do, etc., are all listed later in the "Putting It All Together" section of this book.

DRILL #1: BLOW BUBBLES IN THE WATER

If this seems like something kids learn the first few times they take a swimming lesson, that's the point. We want to simplify every drill so it almost seems too easy. But make no mistake, this drill is extremely effective. Keeping the drills this simple reduces the likelihood of your brain entering fight-or-flight mode so you can stay calm and perform the drill correctly, with perfect form, over and over. Perform pool drills over and over successfully and you'll teach your brain that being in water doesn't mean danger, it's just a regular thing you do.

- Stand in the shallow end of a pool, facing the wall.
- Place your hands on the wall.
- Stick your face in the water, and immediately blow bubbles through your nose or mouth—it doesn't matter which one.
- Blow the air out continuously without stopping. (Try humming while breathing out, which helps make the exhalation consistent and can calm you down.)
- Repeat this over and over.

How to know you've mastered it: When you can stick your face in the water at any time, in any way, at any angle, and your reaction is to blow bubbles immediately, you've mastered this drill. You also know you've mastered this if you stop getting water up your nose. If you're still getting water up your nose, that means there's a point in time when you're holding your breath. Go back and keep blowing bubbles until there's no more water up your nose.

This drill is fairly straightforward but seeing the exact timing of when to start breathing out, how long to breathe out for, and whether the air is coming out your nose or mouth will help you make progress with this drill very quickly. Go to triathlontaren.com/swimfoundations and check out the video.

DRILL #2: SINK DOWNS

This drill can be incorporated throughout the time you're developing your new breathing pattern. You can do it after several repetitions of the Blow Bubbles drill or even during a swim workout to remind your body that as soon as your face enters the water, it's time to exhale.

This drill reinforces to your brain that when your face enters the water, it's exhalation time. It also requires you to become calm and comfortable while you're under the surface of the water.

- Go into the deep end of the pool and face the wall, hanging onto the edge of the pool.

- Let go of the wall and immediately start exhaling.

- You'll start sinking. (If you aren't sinking, blow harder).

- Keep exhaling as you sink, emptying your lungs. (Humming will help you stay calm.)

- Sink down only as far as you can go without feeling a sense of panic.

- Gradually sink down farther and farther, always remaining calm.

- Come back to the surface, regain calmness, and then repeat.

How to know you've mastered it: When you can sink all the way down to the bottom of the pool without a feeling of panic and without getting water up your nose, you've mastered this drill.

When you watch the video for this drill at triathlontaren.com/swimfoundations take a look at how far I'm able to sink down without feeling panicked. You'll easily be able to do this with a small amount of practice, teaching your body to have a huge amount of comfort being underwater.

DRILL #3: BLOW BUBBLES LYING FACEDOWN

This drill is a progression from the Blow Bubbles drill.

- Stand in the shallow end of a pool, facing the wall.

- Place your hands on the wall.

- Stick your face in the water and immediately blow bubbles through your nose or mouth—it doesn't matter which one.

- Kick your feet off the bottom of the pool and allow them to float up until they're in behind you, kicking very gently.

  ○ Your kick should be within a narrow 1.5-foot-wide channel, heels just breaking the surface of the water, toes slightly pointed.

  ○ Kick as lightly as you possibly can while keeping your heels at the surface of the water.

- Blow the air out continuously without stopping.

  ○ Humming while breathing out helps make the exhalation consistent, plus it can help calm you down.

- Keep kicking and blowing bubbles continuously until you run out of air. Then stand back up, reset yourself so you're totally calm again, and then repeat.

How to know you've mastered it: When you can perform this drill without any feeling of panic whatsoever, you've mastered it. Do not move on from this drill if you feel rushed, if you have to kick vigorously, or if water shoots up your nose. Keep doing it until these things no longer happen before you move on.

When you watch the video of this drill from triathlontaren.com/swimfoundations, take special note of how narrow and gentle the kick is. After watching the video several times, try to embed a tempo of the kick in your brain so when you go to the pool you can emulate that gentle kick, saving your oxygen and not feeling out of breath.

DRILL #4: BLOW BUBBLES LYING DOWN AND TURN TO BREATHE

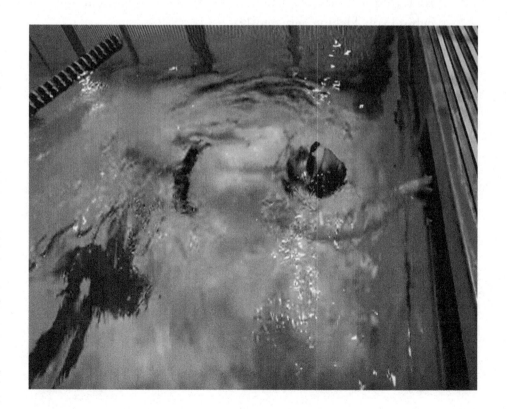

This drill is exactly like the Blow Bubbles Lying Down drill, but now we're going to start incorporating breathing as you would during swimming. Now that you're more comfortable with the basic ability to breathe out with your face in the water, the key focus now will be your new proper breathing pattern.

- Stand in the shallow end of a pool, facing the wall.

- Place your hands on the wall.

- Stick your face in the water and immediately blow bubbles through your nose or mouth—it doesn't matter which one.

- Kick your feet off the bottom of the pool and float them up behind you, kicking very gently.

- Blow the air out continuously without stopping.

- When you feel the need to breathe turn (but DO NOT LIFT) your head to grab a little sip of air.

  - This sip of air is not a gasp or a gulp; it's truly a sip, a tiny little breath. Big gulps of air fill up your chest cavity and encourage that tight, breathless feeling we're trying to avoid.

How to know you've mastered it: When you can perform this drill for upwards of three continuous minutes without a break, you've mastered it. Congrats! At this point, you've built your basic swim breathing pattern.

This drill, while seemingly quite easy, might be challenging to do properly. Watch the video for this drill and the video from the previous drill at triathlontaren.com/swimfoundations and notice the similarities in the tempo of the kick and where the key points of the back of your head, butt, and heels are in relation to the surface of the water.

DRILL #5: CORKSCREW DRILL WITH FINS

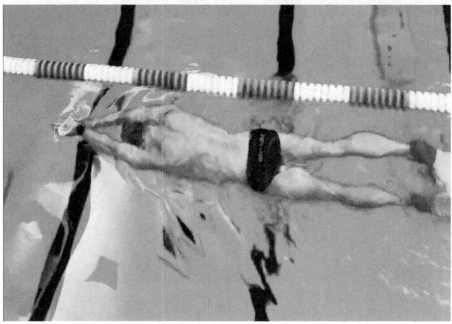

You've now rewired your brain to be comfortable in the water and you've got your breathing pattern dialed in. We'll now start transitioning into movement.

- Put on a pair of flippers. (We strongly encourage you to get the type of flippers we'll recommend later in the gear section.)

- In the shallow end, push away from the wall, facedown with your arms outstretched overhead.

- Kick with the same motion you used in the previous drills:
  - Heels breaking the surface of the water slightly
  - Toes pointed gently
  - Feet within a 1.5-foot-wide channel

- Breathe out continuously until you feel the need to breathe in. Then flip yourself onto your back.

- Once you've grabbed two calm breaths, flip back onto your stomach.

- Repeat this pattern with a flip to the left and then to the right so you're turning both ways.

How to know you've mastered it: When you can perform lap after lap of this drill without feeling out of breath or needing to breathe more than twice while on your back, you've mastered it.

You'll notice, by now, we've got you very close to actual swimming with only this handful of drills. You will have developed a better breathing pattern than a lot of triathletes, and building a head turn rather than a head lift will give you a huge advantage when we move on to Floating Like a Log.

This drill is probably the hardest drill to understand without seeing it. Taking ten seconds to watch the video here, at triathlontaren.com/swimfoundations, will clear everything up. When you watch this video, take note of how the drill forces you to be underwater, potentially causing struggle, but watch how I come back up to the surface of the water. That calmness and surety that you'll come back to the water surface is a critical part of performing this drill properly.

BREATHING FINE PRINT

Before moving on to the next section, we need to address some of the most common questions, around the most common issues, keeping triathletes from mastering their breathing during the swim.

TWO-STROKE BREATHING vs. BILATERAL BREATHING

Most coaches will say bilateral breathing (being able to breathe to both the left and the right) is crucial to successful swimming. They say this makes your stroke balanced and you can see on both sides when swimming in open water with athletes all around you.

Unfortunately, this often gets confused with the belief that triathletes need to swim with a bilateral breathing pattern, taking a breath every three strokes so you breathe to both sides, like this:

Stroke-stroke-stroke, then breathe to the left, stroke-stroke-stroke, then breathe to the right... and repeat.

This bilateral breathing pattern is also called a three-stroke breathing pattern and while it does balance out the stroke, it also reduces the amount of oxygen triathletes receive.

Instead, learning to breathe to both sides but maintaining a two-stroke breathing pattern also balances out the stroke while providing 50 percent more oxygen. We want you to breathe every second stroke, getting in as much oxygen as possible but we want you to switch the side you breathe on every length instead of after the two strokes. You'll still balance your stroke and develop the ability to breathe and sight on both sides.

NOSE CLIPS

When triathletes start swimming, they'll often get water up their noses because they haven't developed the reflex to breathe out as soon as they put their faces in the water. Blowing out has the added benefit of creating a tiny bit of pressure inside the nose, keeping water out. But instead of training their bodies to do this action, lots of people skip the work and go straight to a nose clip.

We don't recommend nose clips because one of the first things we need to accomplish with swim breathing is getting all the CO_2 out of our lungs. Plugging up one of the ways we can expel CO_2 from our bodies doesn't do us any favours.

If you go through the process of developing your breathing mechanics using the process we've outlined, you'll naturally be breathing out the entire time your face is in the water, you'll have that little bit of pressure in your nose, and you won't get water up that honker.

BREATHING THROUGH THE NOSE OR THE MOUTH?

Why can't it be both?

Some coaches say you should breathe out through your nose, some say out through the mouth. Some say in through the nose and out through the mouth or vice versa.

I've recorded video of Lucy Charles, the best female swimmer in IRONMAN triathlon racing, up close and personal in the water. After watching some of that footage in super-slow motion, I noticed bubbles coming out of BOTH her nose and her mouth on nearly every stroke. Watch the footage of just about every elite triathlete and you'll see a similar thing.

The point is, don't stress about whether you should be breathing out of your nose or your mouth. Just breathe out forcefully and get that CO_2 out however you have to.

USING A SNORKEL

I once worked with a triathlete who was having a hard time catching his breath after years of working on his swim. He asked to try my snorkel because he saw me using it so often, figuring it might be the answer.

The athlete swam 25 meters, got out of the pool and walked back. He handed me the snorkel and said, "That thing doesn't work!" I replied, "Give it three weeks, not one length."

Every single new thing we learn in swimming takes about 10 workouts to get the hang of. When swimming three times a week, this means each new thing we learn will take around three weeks to get the hang of. Snorkels are no different.

When you first start using a snorkel, expect it to feel hard. The breathing pattern is new (again), and you're inhaling the little bit of carbon dioxide left in the shaft of the snorkel from your previous exhale. Give it three weeks and it will feel much better.

CHAPTER 3

FLOAT LIKE A LOG

FLOAT LIKE A LOG INTRO

Now that you've got your breathing under control, there's really nothing holding you back from developing excellent swim technique that just putting in tons of laps won't fix. We started with breathing because without getting that nailed down, every triathlete has a little piece of their brain saying, "What do you mean I have to swim with good technique? We're in a crisis situation here. Can't you see we're drowning in water and we need to panic?!"

The purpose of the breathing section was to rewire your brain to accept being in the water. Now that you've trained your body with your new breathing pattern, you'll be ready to spend time on the technical aspects of swimming without your brain putting up a fight. Soon you'll be floating across the pool as smoothly and easily as a log.

I want you to once again picture pushing a smooth, straight log across the surface of water. Easy, right? Now instead of picturing a log, picture a gnarled-up, twisty tree branch and how hard it is to push through the water thanks to the resistance from the twisty limbs.

Forgive me for getting scientific for a second. To move through water, swimmers have four forces they must deal with: gravity from the weight of their body pulling them down, buoyancy from the air in their lungs lifting them up (more on why this isn't such a good thing for us swimmers in a bit), thrust from the swim stroke moving them forward, and drag from the density of the water pushing back on the swimmer.[2]

Of those four forces, thrust is the only one that's really on our side. The rest of the forces work against us:

- Water is 784 times denser than air, so drag from the water slows us down.

- Gravity pulls us down in the water, away from the precious air.

- Buoyancy should help us but unfortunately, the part of the body that's most buoyant (our lungs) is in the upper half of the torso, so our bodies are like seesaws, causing our legs to sink and thus creating more drag.

---

[2] https://www.real-world-physics-problems.com/physics-of-swimming.html

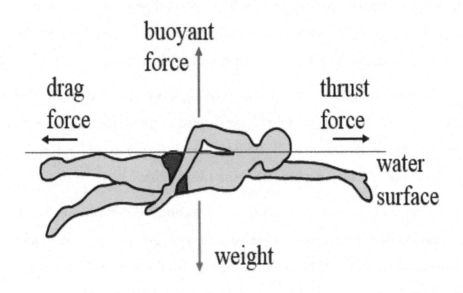

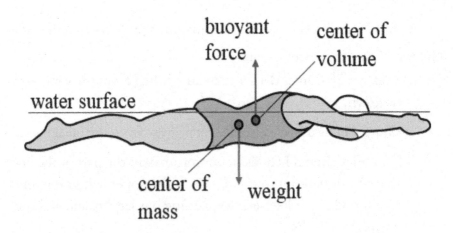

This is where the number-one enemy of floating across the water pops up: the next challenge we have to overcome is sinking legs. The air in the lungs pushes a triathlete's upper body toward the surface of the water but because our centre of mass is closer to our hips, this gets counterbalanced by our legs sinking in the water. Sunken legs cause drag and slow us down, which brings us back to that panic response because we feel like we're getting pulled under the water.

Let's revisit the idea of the log versus the tree branch. The log is like an elite swimmer: straight, close to the surface of the water, looking tall, moving quickly, and not sinking. The tree branch is like the rest of us age-group swimmers: the twigs sticking out under the water are like our sinking legs, causing drag. The other twigs sticking out to the side cause the entire piece of wood to twist and turn; they're like our arms and legs going out to the side, causing even more drag.

We want to turn our bodies into that log. This can be easy with the right technique. Heck, kids learn to do it early on (long before they're anything close to elite swimmers), with the Dead Man's Float drill (what an awful name for a good drill). Masters swimmers can do it too, and you will easily learn how to get your legs up to the surface of the water so you can move quickly and smoothly like that log.

I'm sure a huge number of you are saying, "But, Taren, I played hockey/weight lifted/ran/naturally grew muscular legs [insert other excuse here]. I'm a natural sinker and won't be able to get my legs to float." You know who else has muscular legs? Me. Not convinced? Pro triathlete Cameron Wurf has a lifetime of muscular development in his legs from Olympic-caliber rowing as well as cycling as a professional in the grand tours. He told me once that early in his triathlon career, he also had sinking legs. Yet, in 2018 he came out of the water in the front swim pack at the IRONMAN World Championship in Kona. Still not convinced? Jim Lubinski, pro triathlete and Tower 26 swim coach, was a professional hockey player who is incredibly muscular and looks more like a bulky hockey player than a swimmer, yet he often comes out in the front swim pack.

Everyone, even you with the sinking legs, can learn to float close to the surface of the water like that log and those front-pack swimmers. You just need the right technique which is not hard to develop. It all starts with a little bit of body awareness and finishes with a proper kick. Simple as that.

Now, let's go get those legs up close to the surface of the water.

FLOAT LIKE A LOG TECHNIQUE

Correct swim technique to float like a log looks very simple. In fact, I would say when it's done properly, it's simpler to execute than the wiggly flailing common to a lot of new triathletes. Not you though. With a committed effort on your part, we'll get your technique shipshape in no time and you'll look like this:

1. You'll look straight down at the bottom of the pool so the water line is at the very top of your head.

2. You'll have the back of your head, your butt, and your heels at the surface of the water.

3. Your heels will kick in and out of the surface of the water, keeping your legs from sinking.

If you've done any of the Breathe Like a Dolphin drills, you'll notice similarities between these three points and some of the main points we emphasized in the breathing drills. That's intentional. We want drills to cooperate with each other as one cohesive system.

When we approach the Float Like a Log technique, we have to accomplish a few things:

1. We have to narrow the channel the entire body takes up from the frontal view.
2. We have to conserve energy so we don't use up oxygen or burn out the legs before we get on the bike.
3. We have to make this technique automatic so we can execute it under the pressure of a race.

Common faults that lead to sinking legs:

1. Lifting our heads to breathe, thus driving our legs down.
2. Kicking aggressively and wildly, burning up a huge amount of oxygen and initiating a panic response.
3. Kicking wide or spreading our legs apart as we kick, creating drag outside the body line.

What's the correct technique to create a floating body position?

1. Gently press the chest downward into the water to counteract buoyancy.
2. Slightly tense the core from the belly button all the way down and around to the butt cheeks to allow the legs to seesaw upward as a result of pressing the chest downward.
3. Kick as lightly as possible to have the heels just breaking the surface of the water.
4. Kick in a narrow channel, keeping the legs right in behind the body, reducing drag.

5. Point the toes gently, keeping them right in behind the body, further reducing drag.

Remember, when you get these points nailed down, you'll look like this: the back of your head, your butt cheeks and your heels will be at the surface of the water. You'll be looking straight down at the bottom of the pool. Your legs will be in a channel only about 1.5 feet wide. You'll be turning your head so slightly to breathe that it barely looks like you're catching a breath (kind of like when a dolphin surfaces to breathe).

Enough chatter! Let's build that Float Like a Log technique for you.

FLOAT LIKE A LOG PROGRESSION

DRILL #1 (and 2, and 3, and 4, and. . .): KICKING

"Wait, wait, WAIT, Taren. I thought you said earlier that focusing on kicking isn't really important for triathletes because it isn't going to affect our overall propulsion." Good catch, Trainiac! That's why we don't focus on kicking for propulsion; we use kicking sparingly just as a tool to keep our legs from sinking.

When we created our "How to Swim" online course with professional triathletes Lucy Charles and Reece Barclay, we got to hear how two very different athletes both became elite swimmers and some of the best swimmers in IRONMAN. Lucy took up swimming at an early age so she developed the core stability and body awareness that allows her to swim very fast without kicking much. Meanwhile, Reece took up swimming at a later age so he says he actually has to kick fairly hard to keep his legs up at the surface of the water. Both of them said throughout the entire week of production for our online swim course that they work on their kick not for propulsion but strictly for body position.

There is a downside to relying on the kick to keep our legs at the surface of the water: our legs are big, bulky muscle groups that require a lot of energy and oxygen to power. If we kick too hard, we'll burn through our oxygen stores and undo all that work we did in the first section, likely initiating a panic response. We'll also be very tired by the time we get to our bikes because we've been motoring away on our kick for the entire swim.

What we're going to accomplish with this kick drill progression is building your ability to kick only enough to keep your heels and butt at the surface of the water, and no more. Save yourself for the bike.

EXECUTION OF ALL KICKING DRILLS

The following four kick drills are all executed exactly the same way. The only difference is the level of difficulty required to execute the drill. So I'll provide these points that apply to all of the four kick drills listed below:

- Look straight down at the bottom of the pool.
  - **Special note:** Unlike most kick drills that have your head out of the water (which encourages your legs to sink), in

these drills, your face will be IN the water while you're breathing through a snorkel.

- Keep the back of your head, your butt, and your heels touching the surface of the water.

- Extend your arms out front, shoulder width apart.
  - **For drills with a board,** this means you're holding the butt-end corners of the board on the edge closest to you, NOT the leading edge (or rounded edge) of the board.

- Kick just hard enough to keep your heels breaking the surface of the water slightly and never any harder.

- Kick within a narrow 1.5-foot channel.

- Activate your core to stabilize your upper body. This will prevent the kicking from causing your torso to rock back and forth. DO NOT allow that rocking to happen!

Reminder: the sequence of how to perform these drills with regard to where they should be put in a workout, how many laps of them to do, etc., are all listed later in the book in the "Putting It All Together" section.

Kicking and kick drills are one of the most misunderstood and poorly executed drills that triathletes perform. Make sure you watch the video, perhaps several times, of the entire kick drill sequence at triathlontaren.com/swimfoundations to understand correct and incorrect body posture, the correct way to hold your hands on the kick board, where your eyes should be looking, and more. Get these drills right and you'll make huge progress in your swim. Get them wrong and you could be spending a lot of time kicking and going nowhere.

Progression #1: Kick with Board, Snorkel, and Fins

Progression #2: Kick with Snorkel and Fins (Trainiac Drill)

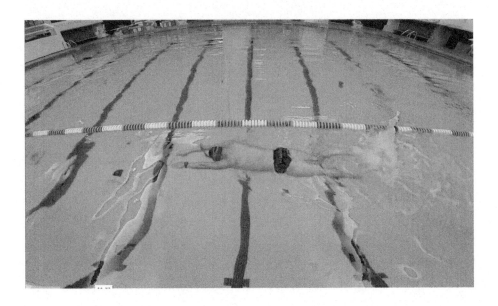

Progression #3: Kick with Board and Snorkel

Progression #4: Kick with Snorkel Only

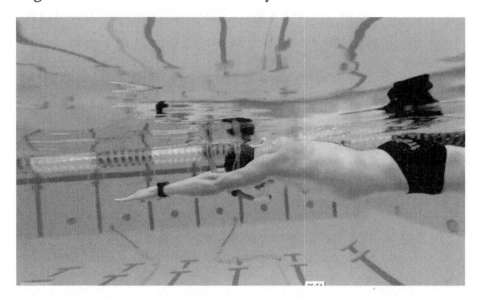

How to know you've mastered it: When you can kick across a 25-yard or meter pool in 45 seconds or less, using just a snorkel, you've mastered this drill progression. (Note: You should spend 8-10 workouts incorporating each drill progression before moving on to the next one.)

The two drills below are another progression of the kick drills we just learned but there are some differences significant enough to warrant a separate section on how to execute these **side** kicking drills. Continue to follow the directions listed above for the kick drill progressions 1--4 in addition to the following:

- For side kicking, your body will be turned 45 degrees NOT 90 degrees (90 degrees is over-rotation and causes the body to wiggle, thus undoing all of the good, firm body positioning we've been working on.)

- One hand is extended straight out front from your shoulder, keeping your fingertips lower than your wrist, which is lower than the elbow, which is lower than the shoulder. This hand is COMPLETELY stationary.

- Chin rests on the shoulder of the extended arm, eliminating the gap between the chin and the shoulder, which creates drag.

Progression #5: Side Kick with Snorkel and Fins

Hand positioning during this drill is the critical thing you'll want to take note of, and you can see exactly what that looks like if you go to triathlontaren.com/swimfoundations. You want to engrain the exact right hand position and stability of that hand. If you don't have your hand in the right position at the start of the swim stroke, it'll be extremely hard to get it back on the right track during the rest of the swim stroke. Watch those videos and hold that hand dead-steady in the right spot.

Progression #6: Side Kick with Fins Only

How to know you've mastered side kicking: When you can complete the Side Kick with Fins Only drill (no snorkel), feeling your heels still break the surface of the water, your extended hand doesn't move around, and you can comfortably breathe without a sense of panic, you've got this drill nailed and you're floating like a log!

FLOAT LIKE A LOG FINE PRINT

SWIMMING "DOWNHILL"

Athletes often hear that they should press their chest, neck, and head deep into the water, which will bring their legs up and give them the feeling of swimming downhill. This advice is a bit extreme for my liking because if athletes can get the back of their head, their butt, and their heels at the surface of the water *without* forcing a "downhill" press, they'll be more relaxed and comfortable. A deep press into the water might also stimulate an unnaturally lower head position, causing an athlete to lift their head to breathe, resulting in sinking legs.

I recommend trying to visualize swimming downhill and seeing how it feels. If it feels natural and not forced, if you don't have to lift your head to breathe, and if you still have a good range of motion, then by all means, use it. Instead, I recommend you feel like leaning forward while standing, and pressing your chest into someone's fist. However, the Float Like a Log drill progression is designed to accomplish the same goal as swimming downhill, but without the risks.

FLOATY PANTS

Neoprene ROKA SIM Shorts

Floaty pants, better known as neoprene swim shorts, are a great tool because they bring an athlete's hips up close to the surface of the water the same way a pull buoy does, while still allowing an athlete to kick. Unfortunately, wearing floaty pants can become a crutch and mask underlying poor body positioning.

You might say your race is a wetsuit swim so the floaty pants are fine because they're similar to how your race conditions will be. That's true only with regard to where your hips sit in relation to the surface of the water, but you still need to develop core tightness to reduce body wiggles. You also need to develop the ability to naturally keep your heels at the surface of the water. There's also going to come a time when you do a race that has a non-wetsuit swim, so you have to be able to do this without the crutch of neoprene keeping you afloat.

I would say floaty pants are a fun "sometimes treat". Use them only during recovery swims that are less focused on doing "work" and more about just enhancing recovery by moving your limbs and getting blood flowing. They're not meant to be used for regular training swims.

PULL BUOY

Common ROKA pull buoy

If floaty pants are a crutch, a pull buoy is a wheelchair. The way most athletes use a pull buoy is one of my biggest pet peeves when it comes to pool swim "aids." Use a pull buoy correctly and it can be one of the best tools available to an age-group triathlete. Use it incorrectly and it can actually amplify the problems of poor alignment and body position that cause athletes to have sinking legs and not be able to float like a log at the surface of the water.

When used by itself, with no other toys like an ankle strap or a snorkel, a pull buoy breaks the body into two parts: your upper body on one side of the pull buoy and your lower body on the other side. When an athlete using just a pull buoy turns their head to breathe, their upper body can be moving one way while their lower body is going the other way. This causes the body to wiggle and creates drag, but the athlete doesn't know this is creating a problem because the pull buoy is artificially creating "good" form by keeping their hips at the surface of the water.

Correct use of a pull buoy will almost always be paired with an ankle strap and a snorkel. This creates a unified body line and forces the athlete to focus on keeping the head, butt, and heels at the surface of the water while maintaining the nice long, unified, solid, log-like body position.

ANKLE BANDS

ROKA ankle band

Ankle bands and pull buoys go together like peanut butter and jelly. We don't ever recommend using a pull buoy without an ankle strap, as it'll force you to treat your entire body as one long unified object, enhancing the Float Like a Log drill progression.

The downside (upside, if you ask me) to the ankle strap is that it doesn't allow you to kick while using the pull buoy. That's kind of the point: we want to take kicking out of the equation and put body positioning at the forefront of our focus. Using a pull buoy and ankle strap together will allow you to feel like you're really using your core to keep your legs at the surface of the water, and it'll cause your legs to sway side to side if you aren't focused on having a nice stiff core.

The pull buoy/band pairing is kind of like a "Take your medicine. It tastes awful, but it's good for you" kind of tool.

TWO-BEAT KICK

A two-beat kick, just one kick for every arm stroke, is great in theory and it looks really cool in videos on social media. In fact, if you look for the video on YouTube titled "Rio Replay: Women's 800m Freestyle Final" and skip forward to 4:56, you'll see a video of Katie Ledecky using a one-beat kick with just a little whip kick for every two arm strokes.

The proponents of this technique say athletes who use a two-beat kick will save oxygen and their legs will be fresher for the bike. I'll just come right out and say it: I believe that's bad advice, and these individuals are targeting unknowing triathletes who don't yet know any better. Sure, in theory, what they're saying makes sense: "You're a new adult swimmer. You probably feel out of breath when you're swimming. Legs are huge muscle groups that require a lot of oxygen. So kick less and you'll have more oxygen." But remember, in section one, we learned that the feeling of being out of breath isn't from a lack of oxygen, it's an improper breathing pattern and a buildup of CO_2.

Here's some #realtalk about the two-beat kick: we know new triathletes aren't great kickers like Katie Ledecky and other elite swimmers. We also know new triathletes more often than not have sinking legs because we don't have the core stability and body awareness that's been developed in elite athletes like Katie Ledecky through tens of millions of meters of swimming from a young age. And finally, we know kicking helps to lift an athlete's legs up closer to the surface, reducing drag and the sensation of sinking.

So telling an athlete to kick less and making them believe it's going to solve their problem is ignoring the real issue of needing to have proper breathing abilities. It's also taking away one of the most important tools an athlete has to get themselves into a good body position: their kick.

If someone tells you that you should be using a two-beat kick, be wary and look to the nearly 0 percent of swimmers who are confident in the water using a two-beat kick.

KICK SETS

Elite swimmers do thousands of meters every week with kicking. Sometimes they do entire workouts just kicking. While we DO use kick sets with our athletes on Team Trainiac, we don't spend enormous amounts of time on kicking like elite swimmers do.

As triathletes, we need our kick to be just strong enough to keep our heels breaking the surface of the water, and no more. Once we've accomplished getting our heels at the surface of the water, our legs are out of the way, so they're not creating drag and we're not sinking anymore. Mission accomplished.

Focusing on kicking for anything other than getting into a good body position is a low return on time invested. As mentioned before, as a triathlete, you might need to kick hundreds of thousands of yards to double the propulsive effect of your kick, but the net increased propulsion might be an additional 2 to 6 percent and it will come at the cost of tired legs for biking and reduced available oxygen.

One last note: If you find yourself in a swim group doing a lot of kicking, definitely feel free to join in but use a snorkel and perform the kicking with your face in the water the way we've done in the drill progression for this section. Don't kick with your head out of the water because that will reinforce sinking legs.

SHOULD YOU FOCUS MUCH ON KICK, IF YOUR RACE IS GOING TO BE A WETSUIT SWIM?

Developing a proper kick that gets your body into a better position in relation to the surface of the water is always a good idea. This skill is one of the basic requirements of being a capable swimmer, so relying on a wetsuit to do the work for you is like saying, "I'm not going to fix this broken leg because I'll be able to take a wheelchair everywhere." The leg is still broken, the wheelchair eventually becomes a cumbersome hassle, and not having fixed your leg in the first place will prevent you from doing a lot of things you want to do in life.

Put in the work in the pool to become a better overall swimmer and those skills will help you be a better triathlete both with and without a wetsuit.

CHAPTER 4

RACE LIKE AN ARROW

RACE LIKE AN ARROW INTRO

By now, you can breathe comfortably in the water and you can stay up close to the water's surface. That puts you a step ahead of the majority of amateur triathletes you'll be racing against. Most importantly though, you're a way better swimmer than when you first started. And we're not even done yet!

The final step to build your foundation for swimming is to make sure all your effort is spent producing forward motion and reducing any movement that sends energy anywhere but straight ahead.

The next time you're at the pool, I want you to find some elite swimmers and watch them swim away from you while they're swimming freestyle. What you're going to see is how straight their body lines are. Elite swimmers' bodies are so aligned that their hips stay directly behind their heads and their feet are directly behind their hips. There's no swaying side to side. Elite swimmers' strokes are also in a narrow channel, typically entering the water and exiting the water in roughly the same channel.

Going back to our old analogy of the log, think about how incredibly easy it is to push a log across the surface of water when it's pointed straight ahead. Now think about how much it would slow down if you were towing the log from the front end while the back end was swaying side to side. Eliminating that side to side movement is the final step in building a solid swim technique foundation.

Swaying side to side can be caused by a lack of core stability and a floppy kick, but we already addressed your kick in the "Float Like a Log" section. And, if you've developed the "Breathe Like a Dolphin" skills to keep your head fixed, and the "Float Like a Log" skills to have a straight body line, the only remaining potential cause for swaying is improper direction of your hands as they enter the water.

All parts of our bodies are connected, so what happens at the front of the stroke affects what happens with the kick. If an athlete lets the buoyancy of their lungs bring their chest up in the water, their legs will sink. Similarly, if a triathlete crosses over the center line of their body when their hand enters the water (more on this soon), it results in an off-setting crossover of the legs to "balance out" the body, but it's an incorrect balancing out.

In this "Race Like an Arrow" section, you'll develop the ability to keep that nice straight body line from the "Float Like a Log" section while breathing with full swim strokes. You'll also know how to keep your hand straight out in front of you as it enters the water and keep it in a straight channel from start to finish, producing enough force to propel you forward.

Like the previous two sections and series of drill progressions, Race Like an Arrow picks up where we left off in the previous section. That's why you need to have mastered all the previous skills before moving on to this next part. If you've been patient and mastered the previous drills, these final drills will seem like an easy final touch on your swimming foundation.

RACE LIKE AN ARROW TECHNIQUE

Correct swim technique to race like an arrow is very simple. Combined with the skills you developed in the first two sections, this will be easy to master because this technique actually minimizes movements. When you're racing like an arrow, you'll look like this:

1. Your head, hips, and feet will stay in a straight line the entire time.

2. Your hand will enter the water between the edge of your head and the outside of your shoulder.

3. While under the water, your hand will travel in a path that stays in the same channel it entered the water (between the edge of your head and the outside of your shoulder).

4. While under the water, the palm of your hand will always face the back wall of the pool.

Those four points are the simple steps we'll work on to tie everything together so you're moving all your energy in a straight line. Forget about the articles you've read describing "the seven phases of the swim stroke," or worrying about the details of "enter-extend-pull-exit-recover." And don't even get me started on the underwater S-pull. That's all too complicated! All you need to do is put your arm into the water straight above your shoulder and pull it straight back.

When we start to approach the Race Like an Arrow technique, we're working to accomplish a few things:

1. We have to keep our hips and feet in a straight line.

2. We have to keep our hands and arms generating force in a straight line.

3. We have to make the movement simple enough that it can be performed under pressure, during a race.

4. We have to make the technique accessible to us stiff adult triathletes who don't have the flexibility of elite swimmers who seem to be made of Silly Putty.

Common faults that lead to swaying side to side (most of which will have been addressed in the "Float Like a Log" section):

1. Lifting the head up to breathe which drives the legs down.

2. A loose core that isn't stiff enough to resist side to side movement.

3. A floppy scissor kick with wide legs that pulls the body side to side.

4. A hand that enters the water, pulls underwater, or exits the water outside of the channel between the edge of the head and the outside of the shoulder.

5. A hand that faces inward or outward, thus pushing water to one side or the other and not directly in behind the athlete.

For those familiar with articles that discuss such fine minutia as "the nine phases of the triathlon swim stroke," our guidelines may sound oversimplified. The reason that the "Race Like an Arrow" technique sounds simple is that it should be simple for age-group triathletes! Elite swimmers' races are decided in hundredths of a second, so they require perfection in every aspect of the stroke and can thus obsess about every single inch of the stroke in great detail. Triathletes don't have such requirements. We need a technique that's easy to replicate over and over while under the stress, and throughout the entire distance, of a race-day swim.

I know from personal experience that perfecting the basics of breathing, floating, and swimming straight are enough to create a very capable swimmer, while having a perfect arm stroke isn't everything it's cracked up to be. In the summer of 2018, I had video analysis done by both Gerry Rodrigues of Tower 26 and Brenton Ford of Effortless Swimming, both of whom said the exact same thing about my swim technique: I was nicely close to the surface of the water, I swam straight, and my arms were aligned, but my pull was almost nonexistent and I was only generating real force in the water for about six inches of my entire arm stroke. Yet, because I had perfected the basics of breathe/float/race straight, the tiny little bit of force I created with my less-than-optimal swim stroke was enough for me to now swim 32 minute half-IRONMANs with ease.

Let's develop that same kind of speed (and hopefully more) for you.

RACE LIKE AN ARROW PROGRESSION

For the hand channel drills below, it'll be hard to know if your hand is in the correct position because so much is moving with your body. The first couple of times you're performing the drill, it helps to have someone on deck watching you from the front or overhead and telling you if you're doing it correctly.

Having someone help you get started with correct execution of the drill is helpful as you don't want to perform hundreds of repetitions of a drill with incorrect form, engraining those bad habits. Even ask a pool employee to watch you for a minute or two if you go to the pool alone!

DRILL #1: HAND CHANNEL SWIMMING WITH SNORKEL AND FINS

When watching the video on this series of hand channel drills at triathlontaren.com/swimfoundations, take note of how the entire arm moves through the water. Watch how the arm makes a "<" and a ">" symbol in the water when viewing from the front. Watch the angle of the arm in relation to the surface of the water. And, take special note of how far back, in relation to the waist, the hand exits.

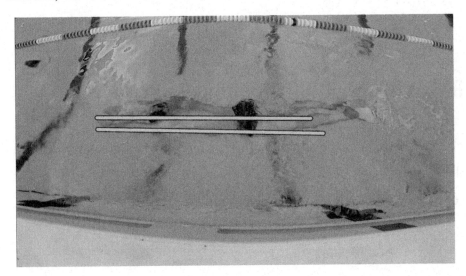

- With fins and a snorkel on, start by doing side kicking: one hand extended directly in front of your shoulder, fingertips lower than your wrist, which is lower than your elbow, which is lower than the shoulder. Your hand stays completely stationary while the other hand is fixed at your side.

- Turn your body to 45 degrees.

- Kick with the back of your head, your butt, and your heels at the surface of the water.

- Look straight down at the bottom of the pool with your chin resting on the shoulder of the extended arm.

- Take full swim strokes with just one arm.

  - Enter in between the edge of your head and the outside of your shoulder.

  - Perform a full stroke with your hand in that same channel, from the edge of your head to the outside of your shoulder, the entire time.

    - ****Any hand movement outside that channel will throw your body offline.****

  - Keep your fingertips pointing to the bottom of the pool and your palm to the back wall for as long as possible, underwater.

How to know you've mastered it: You will likely need a second set of eyes to tell you if you're doing it correctly. Enlist the help of a friend or lifeguard to record you from overhead with a smartphone. (This might feel awkward to ask but in a lot of cases, I've found lifeguards enjoy the break and get interested in what you're doing if they can help in some way.) Alternatively, clamp a camera overhead to record you from the top down. Once you can see that your body is nice and firm, not swaying off a straight line, and your hand is entering and performing the stroke entirely within the hand channel, then you've got this nailed and you'll be swimming dead straight.

DRILL #2: HAND CHANNEL SWIMMING WITH FINS ONLY

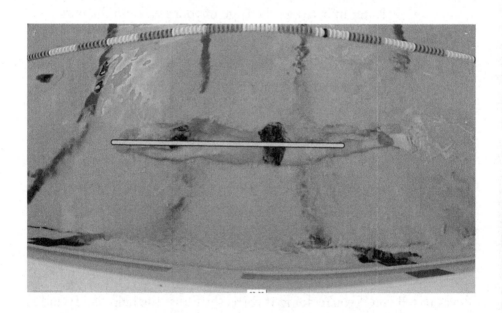

- Maintain all of the above focal points but this time, don't use a snorkel.

- When you breathe, make sure you just turn your head; DO NOT lift your head to breathe.

- Keep one goggle in the water and the waterline should still be in the center.

How to know you've mastered it: Get that same friend/ lifeguard/camera clamp to record you from overhead and from the side. Make sure you've maintained the same straight swimming from the previous drill AND, from the side angle, make sure you're not lifting your head out of the water.

DRILL #3: HAND CHANNEL SWIMMING WITH SNORKEL ONLY

- Maintain all focal points from the previous two drills but this time with no fins.

- You'll have to kick a little harder to keep your legs at the surface of the water.

How to know you've mastered it: When you can execute this drill with the same key points from the previous progressions of the drill, you will have developed an extremely straight swim stroke, be able to breathe, and you'll be positioned at the surface of the water. You're swimming!

The two drills below should put the final polish on your swim stroke. You'll see they're kind of a drill but they're basically just swimming. The system you've been working on in this program has brought you to these final two progressions.

DRILL #4: THREE-STROKES-BREATHE-THREE-STROKES WITH SNORKEL AND FINS

Of all the drills in this book, the next two are probably the ones that cause the most difficulty to understand without seeing them. Make absolutely sure you watch the videos of these drills at triathlontaren.com/swimfoundations because they are the final polish that brings the drills you've been working hard on, all together.

- Push off the wall and side kick for three breaths.

- Take three strokes and you'll find yourself with the other arm extended.

- Side kick for three breaths.

- Take three strokes and you'll find yourself with the other arm extended.

- Repeat.

How to know you've mastered it: When you can comfortably perform this drill without any effort, when you can feel your head, butt, and heels at the surface of the water, and when your arm stroke feels like it's in the proper hand channel, you've mastered it.

DRILL #5: THREE-STROKES-BREATHE-THREE-STROKES WITH FINS ONLY

- Maintain the same focal points from the previous drill.

- Perform the exact same sequence as the previous drill but the breathing pattern changes:

  - ✓ Breathe twice by turning your head (NOT lifting your head).

  - ✓ Take three strokes.

  - ✓ Breathe twice.

  - ✓ Take three strokes.

How to know you've mastered it: When you can perform these drills with the same focal points from the previous drill and it doesn't feel like you're lifting your head (you can test this by making sure you're keeping one goggle in the water), you've got this mastered and your swim stroke is complete!

RACE LIKE AN ARROW FINE PRINT

S-CURVE UNDERWATER (AKA: something you don't need to worry about)

When I was growing up, I heard constantly that when you pulled through the water with your arm, you were supposed to make a swooping S motion. To this day, I still don't really know what that was about because from watching elite swimmers underwater and spending a few hours up close and underwater with top pro triathlete Lucy Charles, I can tell you firsthand that they don't have any distinct swoop. These athletes all follow the basic movement sequence of enter, get their fingertips lower than the wrist, which is lower than the elbow, which is lower than the shoulder, and press back in line with the body.

Elite speed swimmers do certainly have more nuances to their swim strokes; their turnover and body movements are more vigorous because their races are so short, their bodies are much more flexible than age-group triathletes, and they are required to worry about things we age-groupers don't even have to even think about to still be very capable triathlon swimmers.

In fact, if we amateurs try to incorporate an S-pull, there's a good chance it will mess up our mechanics, and that's a risk we don't need to take.

HIGH ELBOW RECOVERY OR STRAIGHT ARM

If you take the "How to Swim with Lucy Charles and Reece Barclay" online course we produced with them on our site protriathlontraining.com, you'll see a significant difference between Lucy's and Reece's arm recoveries as they're swinging their arms back over the water.

Lucy has a very typical straight arm recovery, common to elite open-water swimmers; it's more forceful, allowing the arm to crash through turbulent water, which is the norm in open water. Reece, on the other hand, has a very traditional pool swim stroke with a high elbow recovery that is thought to take pressure off the shoulder. Lucy is the better open-water swimmer while Reece performs better in the pool.

Watch any videos of elite coach Siri Lindley's swim squad and you'll see, almost exclusively, straight arm recoveries. However, watch Lucy Charles's main competition in the water, Lauren Brandon, and you'll see a high elbow recovery.

Both techniques are good, and if you really want to fuss about it, they're not mutually exclusive. During your training, try out what feels better and allows you to maintain a better body position with the key points you've learned in this system. You might even find you can do a high elbow recovery in the pool but your arm becomes straighter when you put on a tight wetsuit.

EARLY VERTICAL FOREARM (AKA: another thing you don't need to worry about)

Early vertical forearm, or EVF, is a swim stroke technique recommended by many elite swim coaches and practiced by many elite speed swimmers. EVF occurs when an athlete enters the water with their arm, extends as far as possible, and then immediately forces their hand downward while keeping their elbow overhead and close to the surface of the water. YouTube search "Ian Thorpe swimming" and you'll see one of the best EVF techniques ever.

The concept of EVF is that by getting the forearm vertical very early in the underwater pull, an athlete has the maximum amount of time they can push water backward with that vertical forearm. This is another concept that is great for elite swimmers with superhuman ranges of motion but it's not a luxury we stiff adult triathletes have, nor is it necessary.

Watch underwater swim footage of Lucy Charles and Josh Amberger, two athletes who consistently come out of the water first among the best fields in IRONMAN. Both of them have a vertical forearm that starts roughly around their head, which is not this insane EVF that everyone talks about being the key.

Gerry Rodrigues, head coach of Tower 26, was an elite swimmer himself and says the EVF concept wasn't even around in his day. He also makes the case that when you remove the improvements in elite swimmers' wall push-offs, EVF swimming isn't really any faster than the non-EVF swimming era. So it's not something we need to bother with (or are even capable of) as amateur, developing triathletes.

CHAPTER 5

PUTTING IT ALL TOGETHER

MAKING CHANGES

The drills and knowledge I've presented here are great, but without also giving you a prescription for when and how to incorporate these things, they aren't much of a system, are they? What I'm going to give to you now is an outline for how I would recommend implementing these drills into your swim program based on where you're at as a swimmer.

We're going to move forward by dividing you into two groups based on your capabilities.

- **Athlete Prescription #1:** You cannot swim 400 meters or yards continuously without a break and/or you feel out of breath at the end of the 400.

- **Athlete Prescription #2:** You can swim 400 meters or yards continuously without feeling out of breath whatsoever after the 400 but still feel like your legs sink, the speed you swim is slower than the effort you put out, or you've never worked on body firmness in the water.

Athletes in group #1 need to reprogram their entire swim technique and build the foundation for swimming from scratch. Athletes in group #2 have a decent amount of comfort in the water but will benefit from better body positioning. You'll be able to determine which category you fall into, in just a moment.

Finally, this is neither exclusively a race-season or offseason drill program; this drill sequence can be done during either the winter or summer months. Regardless of whether you're in Athlete Prescription #1 or Athlete Prescription #2, your largest swim gains will come from developing comfort in the water, so taking this minor step back will leap you many steps forward. The only athletes who should not be doing these drills during the race season are those athletes who are already very comfortable in the water, never feel out of breath, don't feel like they're working terribly hard for good speed, or have an elite swim background or a long history of triathlon swimming behind them (in which case, this probably isn't the guide for them anyway).

ATHLETE PRESCRIPTION #1

Athletes in this group will take a complete step back from their regular swimming workouts and focus solely on the drill progression to break old habits and rewire the brain and body completely. If this is you, I want you to hit pause on doing your own swim workouts or group swim workouts and focus on nothing but this swim drill progression for a short period of time. Don't worry, your regular swim workouts will come back into the picture quickly and you'll be a better swimmer for it.

Swim Session Frequency: At this point, we want to establish good muscle and brain firing patterns, which requires frequency throughout the week. Swimming muscle memory starts dissipating in as little as two days because the water is such an unnatural environment for our human bodies. Try to get into the pool to work on these drills (but only these drills) at least three times a week. Up to five times a week is even better but definitely no more than five.

Swim Session Duration: I would only prescribe those three to five sessions per week for new triathletes if there's a reduced swim session duration. We want frequent reminders for our muscles, but not total overload with big sessions. Swim sessions focused solely on technique can be as short as 10 to 15 minutes, three to five times per week.

Swim Drill Repetitions: When trying something new in the pool, it takes roughly ten sessions to get the hang of it. (This includes new drills, new equipment, new training stimuli, etc.) How fast you progress through these drills, and therefore change your swimming technique entirely, is 100 percent up to you. Perform only two drill sessions per week and it will take five weeks to see any real improvements from a particular drill—that is, if you make progress at all. One to two swim sessions per week is definitely better than nothing but it's still not quite enough to make changes in your muscle firing patterns. Perform three swim sessions per week and you'll absorb the benefits of a drill in about three weeks. Do five swim sessions per week and it'll only take two weeks.

You might do some quick math and think, "Taren has given me 17 drills to work on. Am I going to be doing these drills and no swimming for an entire year?!" Nope, we can overlap, double up, and start incorporating actual swimming into the drills, so you'll make very quick progress, and the time spent just working only on drills will be minimal. Follow the guidelines below for your swim sessions:

- Sessions 1–3:
    - ✓   50% Blow Bubbles
    - ✓   25% Sink Downs
    - ✓   25% Blow Bubbles Facedown
- Sessions 4–6:
    - ✓   25% Blow Bubbles
    - ✓   25% Sink Downs

✓   50% Blow Bubbles Facedown

- Sessions 7–10:

  ✓   25% Sink Downs

  ✓   50% Blow Bubbles Facedown

  ✓   25% Blow Bubbles and Turn to Breathe

- Sessions 11–13:

  ✓   50% Blow Bubbles and Turn to Breathe

  ✓   25% Corkscrew

  ✓   25% Side Kick with Fins

- Sessions 14–16:

  ✓   10% Blow Bubbles and Turn to Breathe

  ✓   40% Corkscrew

  ✓   40% Side Kick with Fins

  ✓   10% Kick with Snorkel/Board/Fins

- Sessions 17–20:

  ✓   10% Corkscrew

  ✓   30% Side Kick with Fins

  ✓   30% Kick with Snorkel/Board/Fins

  ✓   30% Kick with Snorkel/Fins (Trainiac Drill)

- Sessions 21–23:

  ✓ 25% Kick with Snorkel/Board/Fins

  ✓ 50% Kick with Snorkel/Fins (Trainiac Drill)

  - Perform this drill as one-length drill, one-length swim, trying to swim with the same touch-points you focus on during the drill (look down; back of head, butt, and heels at the surface of the water; limit rocking side to side with the upper body).

  ✓ 25% Kick with Board/Snorkel

- Sessions 24–26:

  ✓ 50% Kick with Snorkel/Fins (Trainiac Drill)

  - Perform this drill as one-length drill, one-length swim, trying to swim with the same touch points you focus on during the drill

  ✓ 25% Kick with Board/Snorkel

  ✓ 25% Kick with Snorkel Only

  - Perform this drill as one-length drill, one-length swim, trying to swim with the same touch points you focus on during the drill

- Sessions 27–30:

  ✓ 25% Kick with Board/Snorkel

  ✓ 25% Kick with Snorkel Only

- Perform this drill as one-length drill, one-length swim, trying to swim with the same touch points you focus on during the drill

✓ 25% Side Kick with Snorkel/Fins

- Perform this drill as one-length drill, one-length swim, trying to swim with the same touch points you focus on during the drill

✓ 25% Hand Channel Swimming with Snorkel/Fins

- Perform this drill as one-length drill, one-length swim, trying to swim with the same touch points you focus on during the drill

- Sessions 31–33:

✓ 30% Side Kick with Snorkel/Fins

- Perform this drill as one-length drill, one-length swim, trying to swim with the same touch points you focus on during the drill

✓ 30% Hand Channel Swimming with Snorkel/Fins

- Perform this drill as one-length drill, one-length swim, trying to swim with the same touch points you focus on during the drill

✓ 30% Hand Channel Swimming with Fins

- Perform this drill as one-length drill, one-length swim, trying to swim with the same touch points you focus on during the drill

✓ 10% Hand Channel Swimming with Snorkel

- Sessions 34–36:

  ✓ 30% Side Kick with Fins

  - Perform this drill as one-length drill, one-length swim, trying to swim with the same touch points you focus on during the drill

  ✓ 30% Hand Channel Swimming with Snorkel/Fins

  - Perform this drill as one-length drill, one-length swim, trying to swim with the same touch points you focus on during the drill

  ✓ 30% Hand Channel Swimming with Fins

  - Perform this drill as one-length drill, one-length swim, trying to swim with the same touch points you focus on during the drill

  ✓ 10% Hand Channel Swimming with Snorkel

- Sessions 37–40:

  ✓ 25% Side Kick with Fins

  - Perform this drill as one-length drill, one-length swim, trying to swim with the same touch points you focus on during the drill

  ✓ 50% Three-Strokes-Breathe-Three Strokes with Snorkel/Fins

  ✓ 25% Three-Strokes-Breathe-Three Strokes with Fins

- Sessions 41–43:

    ✓ 50% Three-Strokes-Breathe-Three Strokes with Snorkel/Fins

    - Perform this drill as one-length drill, one-length swim, trying to swim with the same touch points you focus on during the drill

    ✓ 50% Three-Strokes-Breathe-Three Strokes with Fins

    - Perform this drill as one-length drill, one-length swim, trying to swim with the same touch points you focus on during the drill

Notice how, as the sessions progress, the drills become more similar to full swimming. And, as the sessions progress, we mix in more full swimming with the drills. It ends up being a quite a short amount of time you'll spend focusing just on drilling because we don't want to train you to become a good driller; we want you to become a good triathlete, and triathletes swim.

Total time estimate to transform your swim based on frequency of swim sessions:

Swim session per week	1	2	3	4	5
Time to complete entire swim progression	43 wks.	21.5 wks.	14 wks.	11 wks.	8.5 wks.

If you're reading this book, I have to imagine you're in your off-season with several months to get ready for your first race or your next race of the season. If you commit to taking this small pause in your swim workouts and get in just three to five very short drill sessions each week, you'll transform your swimming for the rest of your life in approximately two to three months. In swimming time, two or three months to make huge improvements in your comfort and technique in the water is warp speed and it'll be the fastest progress you'll ever make.

ATHLETE PRESCRIPTION #2

Triathletes in this group must be able to swim 400 meters or yards nonstop without any big "cheater" breaths each time they push off the wall, and they can do so without feeling tired whatsoever when they finish. Be honest with yourself about this! If you think you can complete this 400 test but you get even just a little bit of anxiety when you see a 400 or longer interval in a swim set, you'll be best to go with Prescription #1.

Athletes in the Prescription #2 group will weave the drill sequence in with their swimming more than triathletes in Prescription #1 because group #2 athletes don't need to break their breathing-pattern brain wiring with a full step back from swim workouts.

Swim Session Frequency: Swimming twice per week is enough for a developing triathlete to see moderate improvement, three times per week is ideal, and four times per week will start getting into diminishing returns.

Swim Session Duration: Duration of swim workouts is dependent on the distance of race you're training for. Below are swim durations we utilize for athletes on Team Trainiac:

- Sprint: One endurance swim per week of 20-35 minutes, other swims can be 15-25 minutes.

- Olympic: One endurance swim per week of 40-50 minutes, other swims can be 25-40 minutes.

- 70.3: One endurance swim per week of 60-75 minutes, other swims can be 40-50 minutes.

- Full IRONMAN: One endurance swim per week of 60-90 minutes, other swims can be 40-50 minutes.

Rather than dedicate the entire swim workout exclusively to swim drills, athletes in Prescription #2 should dedicate the first five minutes of every swim session to the prescribed drills to remind the body what good technique is, then move into their swim workout warm up incorporating the drills in the sequence below. For example, this is how a workout would start:

- Spend five minutes of dedicated time spent on Blow Bubbles, Sink Downs, and Blow Bubbles Facedown.

- Warm up with Blow Bubbles Facedown for five seconds, take a small short breath, push off the wall, and swim a 50 very easy. Repeat until warm up is completed.

- Proceed with your workout.

Swim Drill Repetitions: Prior to starting your swim workout, perform five minutes of dedicated drills.

- Sessions 1–3:

    ✓ 50% Blow Bubbles

    ✓ 25% Sink Downs

    ✓ 25% Blow Bubbles Facedown

        - During the warm-up of your swim workout, perform the Blow Bubbles drill for ten seconds, and then immediately go into swimming an easy 50, focusing on blowing out forcefully as you did with the drill.

- Sessions 5–6:

    ✓ 25% Blow Bubbles

    ✓ 25% Sink Downs

    ✓ 50% Blow Bubbles Facedown

        - During the warm-up of your swim workout, perform the Blow Bubbles Facedown drill for 10 seconds then immediately go into swimming an easy 50, focusing on blowing out forcefully as you did with the drill.

- Sessions 7–10:
    - ✓ 25% Sink Downs
    - ✓ 50% Blow Bubbles Facedown
    - ✓ 25% Blow Bubbles and Turn to Breathe
        - During the warm-up of your swim workout, perform the Blow Bubbles Facedown drill for 10 seconds then immediately go into swimming an easy 50, focusing on blowing out forcefully as you did with the drill.

- Sessions 11–13:
    - ✓ 50% Blow Bubbles and Turn to Breathe
    - ✓ 25% Corkscrew
    - ✓ 25% Side Kick with Fins
        - During the warm-up of your swim workout, perform 25 (or 50 if your pool is long course) of the Corkscrew drill, then immediately go into swimming an easy 25 (or 50 if your pool is long course), focusing on a stable body as you did with the drill.

- Sessions 14–16:
    - ✓ 10% Blow Bubbles and Turn to Breathe
    - ✓ 40% Corkscrew
    - ✓ 40% Side Kick with Fins

   ✓ 10% Kick with Snorkel, Board, and Fins

- During the warm-up of your swim workout, perform 25 (or 50 if your pool is long course) of the Side Kick with Fins drill, then immediately go into swimming an easy 25 (or 50 if your pool is long course), focusing on a stable body as you did with the drill.

- Sessions 17–20:

   ✓ 10% Corkscrew

   ✓ 30% Side Kick with Fins

   ✓ 30% Kick with Snorkel, Board & Fins

   ✓ 30% Kick with Snorkel & Fins (Trainiac Drill)

- During the warm-up of your swim workout, perform 50 Kick with Snorkel, Fins, and Board drill, then immediately go into swimming an easy 50, focusing on a stable body as you did with the drill.

- Sessions 21–23:

- 25% Kick with Snorkel, Board, and Fins

- 50% Kick with Snorkel & Fins (Trainiac Drill)

- 25% Kick with Board and Snorkel

- During the warm-up of your swim workout, perform 50 Kick with Snorkel and Fins drill, then immediately go into swimming an easy 50, focusing on a stable body as you did with the drill.

- Sessions 24–26:

  - ✓ 50% Kick with Snorkel and Fins (Trainiac Drill)

  - ✓ 25% Kick with Board and Snorkel

  - ✓ 25% Kick with Snorkel Only

    - During the warm-up of your workout, perform 50 Trainiac Drill, then immediately go into swimming an easy 50, focusing on a stable body as you did with the drill.

- Sessions 27–30:

  - ✓ 25% Kick with Board and Snorkel

  - ✓ 25% Kick with Snorkel Only

  - ✓ 25% Side Kick with Snorkel and Fins, 25% Hand Channel Swimming with Snorkel and Fins

    - During the warm-up of your workout, perform 50 Side Kick with Snorkel and Fins drill, then immediately go into swimming an easy 50, focusing on a stable body as you did with the drill.

- Sessions 31–33:

  ✓ 30% Side Kick with Snorkel and Fins

  ✓ 30% Hand Channel Swimming with Snorkel and Fins

  ✓ 30% Hand Channel Swimming with Fins

  ✓ 10% Hand Channel Swimming with Snorkel

    - During the warm-up of your workout, perform 50 Hand Channel Swimming with Snorkel and Fins drill, then immediately go into swimming an easy 50, focusing on keeping your hand in the proper position as you did with the drill.

- Sessions 34–36:

  ✓ 30% Side Kick with Fins

  ✓ 30% Hand Channel Swimming with Snorkel and Fins

  ✓ 30% Hand Channel Swimming with Fins

  ✓ 10% Hand Channel Swimming with Snorkel

    - During the warm-up of your workout, perform 50 Hand Channel Swimming with Fins drill, then immediately go into swimming an easy 50, focusing on keeping your hand in the proper position as you did with the drill.

- Sessions 37–40:
  - ✓ 25% Side Kick with Fins
  - ✓ 50% Three-Strokes-Breathe-Three-Strokes-Breathe with Snorkel and Fins
  - ✓ 25% Three-Strokes-Breathe-Three-Strokes-Breathe with Fins
    - During the warm-up of your workout, perform 50 Three-Strokes-Breathe-Three-Strokes with Snorkel and Fins drill, then immediately go into swimming an easy 50, focusing on keeping your hand in the proper position as you did with the drill.

- Sessions 41–43:
  - ✓ 50% Three-Strokes-Breathe-Three-Strokes-Breathe with Snorkel and Fins
  - ✓ 50% Three-Strokes-Breathe-Three-Strokes with Fins
    - During the warm-up of your workout, perform 50 Three-Strokes-Breathe-Three-Strokes-Breathe with Fins drill, then immediately go into swimming an easy 50, focusing on keeping your hand in the proper position as you did with the drill.

After completing the five minutes of dedicated drills and the warm-up, your body will be primed to execute your swim workout with good technique. But, don't forget to be conscious of that technique while you're swimming. During the easier efforts in your workout, try to consciously think about incorporating the key points executed during the main drill that you did during the warm-up. Don't bother trying to do this during your efforts at 85 percent swim effort or faster; just focus on swimming fast.

RACE DAY

The system you've just learned should get you to the start line of your next race feeling confident and free of many common triathlon swimming faults, though experience tells me you're still going to have a lot of questions about how to actually execute your swim. In this section, we'll address the most common questions triathlon swimmers have with regard to race day. I'll share the top gear to buy, where to line up at the start line, and how to strategize to allow the work you've done in the pool to show itself in the race.

WETSUITS AND SWIMSKINS

ROKA Maverick Pro Wetsuit

ROKA Viper Pro Swimskin

Developing triathletes often ask if a wetsuit is worth it and which wetsuit they should buy.

Yes, a wetsuit is 100 percent worth it! Wetsuits are buoyant so wearing one will make you faster and give you some confidence, knowing you won't sink. Wetsuits also provide warmth; believe it or not, being in water without a wetsuit actually strips your body of energy/heat, no matter how warm that water is. While training for those marathon swims I did, my training partners and I had to build up to five-hour swims in the pool; we would purposely choose a pool that's always kept at 80 degrees (which is quite warm), and yet, we'd still end the workout shivering because of the heat loss. A wetsuit will make you faster, safer, and warmer—if you choose the right one.

Triathletes should always use a sleeved wetsuit because sleeveless wetsuits expose the armpits which is where a huge amount of heat escapes while swimming. In order to make sure the wetsuit sleeves and shoulders don't constrict your movement, pick a wetsuit that's tight in the body, without any areas that can carry excess water, but also large enough so you can bunch up a little extra neoprene in the shoulder area.

I don't recommend renting a wetsuit because, well . . . eww! There are two types of wetsuits: wetsuits that have been peed in and brand-new wetsuits that are about to be peed in. A developing triathlete doesn't need a super-expensive wetsuit, so you can purchase an inexpensive one for close to the same price as renting one. Then, if you decide you don't want to continue with triathlon or you want to upgrade, you can always sell your inexpensive wetsuit for close to what you paid.

Inexpensive wetsuits are very tough and last a long time. The wetsuit I recommend for new triathletes is the base-level, sleeved XTERRA wetsuit which you can find on Amazon for around US$150. This is the wetsuit I used for my first four years in triathlon and I ended up selling it for $100 after using it in more than a dozen races.

If you're in a warm-water race, wetsuits may not be allowed. If that's the case, you'll have to decide between using a swim skin and just going in your swimsuit.

Swim skins are made of tight, almost-stiff material that compresses your body and wicks water over the surface of the swim skin. They are not buoyant and are just slightly warmer than going without a swim skin. In my testing, swim skins only make triathletes a couple of seconds faster per 100 meters; they are definitely not game changers. One of the biggest benefits of swim skins for developing triathletes is that they force a stiffer body position, resulting in less leg sinking. If money is no object to you, or if you have a huge issue with sinking legs, a swim skin might be a good decision but it's not required.

The wetsuit versus non-wetsuit decision is always made by the race organizers on the morning of the race. The decision is based on a ratio of water temperature to air temperature. To determine if your next race requires a wetsuit or is non-wetsuit, you can look at the online race information (where they'll often say what past races have allowed), you can contact the organizing committee, or look at old race photos to see what triathletes were wearing in previous years of the race. If the race even has a small chance of being a wetsuit race, bring the wetsuit! You'd rather have the wetsuit and not need it than need it and not have it.

WHAT TO WEAR UNDER THE WETSUIT

There are a multitude of different combinations of what you could wear during your first several triathlons. We'll try to cover the most common choices and recommend alternatives for what you use in the swim.

Triathlon Race Kit: If you're wearing a wetsuit or swim skin, the tri kit can go right under the suit. If you're not wearing a wetsuit or swim skin, male triathletes should swim with just the bottoms on because the top will likely create a fair bit of drag in the water. You'll have to put your tri top on in transition and this will be difficult when you're wet, so make sure to practice this in training.

Cycling Kit: If you're wearing a wetsuit or swim skin, the cycling kit can go right under the suit or skin. If you're not wearing a wetsuit or swim skin, male athletes might want to consider wearing tighter swim trunks and no top during the swim; cycling tops will grab a lot of water which creates drag, and most cycling shorts have a big chamois that will soak up water and create an enormous amount of drag. Again, you'll have to put your cycling kit on in transition and this will be difficult when you're wet, so practice this in training.

Running Shorts and Shirt: If you're wearing a wetsuit or swim skin, running shorts can go right under the suit but I'd put the top on in transition so you're not on the bike with a wet, heavy, floppy shirt that might not dry as easily as a tight top. If you're not wearing a wetsuit or swim skin, males might want to consider wearing tighter swim trunks and no top during the swim; running tops will grab a lot of water, creating drag, and all running shorts will basically be an anchor dragging you backward in the swim. Again, you'll have to put your running clothes on in transition and this will be difficult when you're wet, so once again, practice this in training.

WARM UP

If you're able to get in the water before the race, DO IT! This is the best thing you can do before your race to reduce any panic at the swim start and it's more important than a cycling or running warm-up. Warming up in the water before the race will lower your initial heart rate spike at the start of the swim. This should quell some inadvertent panic and you'll be fresher for the rest of the race.

A 5- to 10-minute swim is more than enough to get the heart rate up. Here's a pre-race warm-up I'd recommend:

- 3 minutes of easy swimming

- 5 strokes fast, 25 strokes easy

- 10 strokes fast, 20 strokes easy

- 15 strokes fast, 15 strokes easy

- 20 strokes fast, 10 strokes easy

- 25 strokes fast, 5 strokes easy

***If your swimming warm-up is a full 10 minutes, also do this:

- 20 strokes fast, 10 strokes easy

- 15 strokes fast, 15 strokes easy

- 10 strokes fast, 20 strokes easy

- 5 strokes fast, 25 strokes easy

Your heart rate should be elevated and your body will be warmed up. Then try to stay active as you're waiting for the race to start; bounce around on your toes, do some calisthenics, and just keep your heart rate slightly elevated and your body loose without tiring yourself out.

If you don't have access to the water before the race, it's critical to get warm before the swim start. Unfortunately, not having access to the water for a warm-up is becoming the norm at a lot of IRONMAN branded races; in these races, you're also not allowed to take your bike out of transition once it's checked in so it's even harder to get a really good warm-up. In this case, go through the following checklist to get your body activated for the race and reduce the shock placed on your body at the start of the race:

- While in transition, use TheraBands or StretchCordz to simulate the swim stroke and activate the muscles you'll use during the swim. Start out light and gradually increase speed, performing a total of 3–5 minutes of exercises.

- After you've put on your wetsuit, go down to the water as early as possible and get the lay of the land. If other people are in the water, that's a pretty good sign it's permitted.

  - If you're totally unable to get in the water, at the very least, go to the water's edge to splash some water in your face and down your wetsuit to get rid of that initial shock response. Doing this will drastically reduce the likelihood of a panic response when the race starts.

PRO TIP DIRECTLY FROM TWO-TIME KONA CHAMPION PATRICK LANGE:

- If the morning air or the water is cold, you don't want to get cold before the race start so make sure someone on your support crew has a thermos of warm water so you can put a few cups of that warm water down your wetsuit.

- While waiting to start, don't stay stationary. Bounce around, and shake out your legs and arms.
- Keep your heart rate just slightly elevated so you're warm when you hit the water and the blood is already in your muscles, ready to work.

OTHER TIPS TO STAY WARMER: Some athletes like using swimming ear plugs which they feel can reduce the heat loss a little bit in a cold swim. And double-capping (wearing two swim caps at once) can help keep your head a bit warmer too.

SWIM START POSITIONING

Mass Start for Athletes Who ARE NOT YET Comfortable in the Water:

For athletes who are still not entirely confident in open water, reducing the likelihood of getting jostled around in the chaos of the swim is critically important. Getting jostled around often gets newer triathletes thrown off their rhythm, potentially having to take a break mid-swim and sometimes even having to be pulled out of the water.

There are a couple of things these athletes can do to avoid this happening:

1) They can line up at the very side of the swim start, letting the entire pack swim clustered together while they swim off to the side, away from the chaos; or

2) They can start at the back and let the main group swim away for about five seconds after the start of the race, and then start swimming.

In both cases, the loss of time is minimal. At Kona, for example, if you were to start as far to the left of the start line as possible, you'd only have to swim about two feet farther than everyone swimming down the buoys, in the chaos. If you wait five seconds after the gun goes off before starting your swim, you're likely going to be swimming the majority of the race on your own, so you can get into a groove and not have to stop at all. This will be way faster than if you have to stop and take a break mid-swim because you got caught up in the chaos of the giant pack.

Mass Start for Athletes Who ARE Comfortable in the Water:

For athletes who are comfortable in open water and have practiced swimming with people around them, you may get some benefit from positioning yourself at the start line, in the mix of all the athletes and getting a draft.

However, unless you're swimming around 35 minutes or faster for a half-IRONMAN, or a 1:10 or faster for a full IRONMAN, the benefit of a draft is fairly minimal. Also, quite often people will draft blindly without knowing if the people they're drafting off of are swimming in a straight line down the course.

Unless you're looking for the absolute fastest time possible, you know how to draft in a pack of athletes, and you know how to sight, the time savings you'll get from being in a pack is minimal enough that you might be better off swimming your own race by starting slightly off to the side of the main swim pack.

Wave or Rolling Start:

More and more IRONMAN races are going toward a wave start or rolling start. I think this is fantastic because it adds a level of safety and reduces the intimidation factor. However, it does add another level of planning when you don't have a mass start.

With the wave or rolling start, athletes need to seed themselves in a starting position that is in line with the swim time they expect to have. There are signs at the swim start indicating the approximate times of athletes seeding themselves around those signs. My recommendation is to seed yourself one to three minutes faster than your expected swim time. In a best-case scenario, you'll end up in a slightly faster pack of swimmers and get a small draft. In a worst-case scenario, the group you start with will get away from you fairly quickly, so you'll have fewer athletes bumping around you and you'll get to swim your own race.

SWIM PACK POSITIONING

Once the swim starts, you'll have to make some decisions about how you approach the swim with regard to swimming in a pack or swimming on your own.

As I mentioned before, the benefit of being in a drafting pack is actually pretty limited for most amateur athletes. Getting into a pack, you have to weigh maybe being a tiny little bit faster with the help of a pack, outweighed by the potential for getting knocked around and swimming off course. Unless you're in the top 10 percent of the swimmers in the field, you're probably better off swimming your own race and not worrying about trying to find a draft pack.

If you are one of the fast swimmers, here are guidelines for how to make sure you get the benefit of swimming in a pack without suffering the downsides:

- The fastest spot to draft isn't directly in behind a swimmer. It's just off to the side with your hand entering the water in behind the swimmer's hip.

- Drafting doesn't mean you don't have to think about sighting. The average age-group triathlete only sights once every 20 to 30 strokes while the average elite, open-water swimmer will sight once every six to eight strokes. Odds are, most swimmers you might try to draft off of are swimming off course. So draft as long as the athlete in front of you is swimming a straight line, but it's realistically more important to follow what your own sighting is telling you.

Most athletes won't get a huge benefit from drafting in a pack so, for these athletes, it's best to start at the edge of the start line in a mass swim start, or during a rolling start, immediately swim off to one of the sides. Doing this will make sure you can swim your own race and won't get knocked around.

KICKING HARD AT THE END OF THE SWIM

There is a lot written online and in triathlon publications recommending that in the final 100 or 200 meters of the swim, triathletes kick extra hard to get blood in their legs. This is a ridiculous suggestion. Here's why:

The few seconds after we stand up at the end of the swim to run into transition is a very awkward time for our bodies. We need to reroute our blood from being in our upper bodies and arms as we lie horizontally in the water, to being in our legs as we run with our bodies upright. The act of simply getting out of the water and using your legs to move, places a demand on the body that is going to spike your heart rate. If you've already jacked up your heart rate by kicking extra hard at the end of the swim, you might end up with such a serious heart rate spike that it'll take you 10 to 20 minutes at the start of the bike to get your heart rate under control.

Instead, what we prescribe for Team Trainiac athletes who are quite comfortable in the water is doing deck-ups during swim workouts leading up to a race. A deck-up is doing swimming a specific workout and then quickly climbing out of the water and standing upright or jogging on deck to train the body to reroute the blood flow very quickly. This allows your body to develop an ability to finish the swim without having a big heart rate spike, and you'll be able to get on the bike calmly and attack it right away.

TRAINING FINE PRINT

As you move forward beyond this program and start using more Team Trainiac swim instruction, or even if you're using swim instruction from a group or another coach, there will be a lot of things you'll have questions about. This section is going to address some of the most common things you'll encounter over the course of your swimming career.

Of course, this is just one person's opinion on all of these topics which is based specifically on an understanding of how to develop an age-group triathlete into a proficient swimmer, but there are many ways to swim and you're going to hear a lot of different methods. At the very least, this section will give you a foundation of knowledge through which you can filter some of the information you're going to hear.

DRILLS

We do drills intentionally and sequentially rather than use drills as a band-aid to fix a specific weakness. For example, let's say a coach spots an athlete needing a better high elbow catch underwater (where the fingertips are lower than the wrist, which is lower than the elbow, which is lower than the shoulder), so they prescribe a drill where the athlete doesn't actually take any strokes. Instead, the athlete goes back and forth in the pool, just bending their elbow, doing the start of the stroke with proper form. The thought is that by doing a certain movement over and over, hundreds of times, the movement will make its way into the regular swim stroke. Unfortunately, that's not what happens.

The athlete does the bent-elbow catch drill for hundreds of meters in dozens of workouts but never actually does a drill to incorporate that movement into a real swim stroke. Then, under the pressure of a race, the athlete goes back to their normal swim stroke and they haven't made any improvements.

HOW TO INCORPORATE DRILLS

We like drills and we use them extensively. But as you can see in this booklet, our use of drills is part of an overall system where each drill is a part of a bigger process. The drills lean on each other and build upon themselves.

You'll also see from this booklet that our drills don't isolate one part of the stroke. Rather, they mimic and progress toward a full stroke as quickly as possible, as the athletes make a meaningful change in their swimming.

When there is a specific fault we want to fix in an athlete's stroke, we still prescribe specific drills that are unique to that athlete but we incorporate them into workouts differently than a lot of other coaches do. Most coaches will have a big chunk of the workout, say 300–600 yards or meters dedicated to a single drill or a few drills lumped together. We prefer to prescribe just one drill, the single drill we want an athlete to focus on for a long time, and we execute that drill during the warm-up of their workout, doing 25 drill then immediately going into 25 swim (or 50 drill, 50 swim depending on the pool length or the type of drill).

There are several reasons we incorporate drills this way:

1. Doing the drills at the very start of the workout prevents the athlete from starting a workout enforcing old, bad technique.

2. Doing drills at the start of the workout sets the tone for the technique the athlete wants to use for the rest of the workout.

3. Most importantly, going from the drill immediately into swimming forces the athlete to perform the drill and then instantly swim with a full stroke, trying to mimic the sensations they experienced while doing the drill. This is the only way to actually start making changes to an athlete's stroke that will withstand the pressures of race day.

DRILLS TRIATHLETES SHOULD BE CAUTIOUS OF

There are a few drills that, while they might be beneficial for elite swimmers, can be very detrimental to age group triathletes. These are the main drills to be wary of:

*   Catch-up Drill (front quadrant swimming, any drill focused on increasing the glide): The catch-up drill encourages having both arms overhead at the same time to create a gliding effect. This works fine for elite swimmers who put out a massive amount of power with each stroke, generating enough force to shoot them a long distance forward. Amateur swimmers simply don't have that kind of power, so when they have both hands over the top of their

heads, neither one pressing back in the water, they're decelerating and losing momentum. Every subsequent swim stroke has to get the triathlete restarted at moving forward. This is a clunky and inefficient way to swim. Waves and currents in open water can also throw an athlete off their rhythm which happens easily during a "glide."

- Kicking with Your Head Out of the Water: As we discussed earlier in this book, kicking with your neck craned up and your head out of the water encourages your legs to sink and develops poor body positioning. All kick drills for triathletes should be done with a snorkel, face pointed straight down to the bottom of the pool, and the heels just breaking the surface of the water.

- Head-up Front Crawl (aka: water polo swimming): Although triathletes can technically sight in open water by using water polo-style swimming (taking many strokes in a row with their head out of the water, looking forward) it's not advised. The same way kicking with your head out of the water drives your feet down, water polo swimming will also cause your legs to sink.

- Side Kick Drills: Side kicking drills without fins or a snorkel are some of the hardest things for triathletes to do in the water. Side kicking ends up creating a feeling of sinking and panic, which leads to the dreaded craned neck and lifted head, further causing sinking legs. Side kick drills should only be done with fins and a snorkel at all times.

SWIM GROUPS AND SWIM COACHING

Swimming with a group or getting a coach works for some but a lot of triathletes find it's just not the answer for them. There was a two-year period when I religiously swam with an organized group, three or four times a week, putting in upward of 20,000 meters per week but I was actually getting slower because the structure of those workouts ultimately wasn't what I needed.

Now, I'm not saying swim groups or coaches are inherently bad but not all swim groups and coaches are suitable for all swimmers. If you join a club or hire a coach, look for a group that is known for working with AND GETTING RESULTS for triathletes at your level.

A couple of resources I often highly recommend for age-group triathletes are the Tower 26 online swim program and the Effortless Swimming online swim correction service. I used both for my own training in the past and saw measurable results in just a couple of short months. Of course, I also get some messages about how my Triathlon Taren swim coaching products are great for developing triathletes too, just saying. ;)

SIGHTING/CATCH AND PULL/PACING/SEASON PERIODIZATION

Sighting, the catch-and-pull phase of the stroke, correct pacing and effort levels, and season periodization are all important aspects of a proper swim training program but they're certainly more advanced skills.

I've intentionally left these topics out because the goal of this book is to develop a solid foundation for swimming without getting lost among the dozens of things you can worry about down the road.

Are these other things important? Sure! Are they things a new triathlon swimmer who is focusing on developing comfort in the water should be worried about? Not right now.

If you work your way through this system and continue racing triathlons, these topics will be part of your next steps (and perhaps the foundation for my next swim book). For now, you're going to get the best return on your time spent working on the basics, which is the system you've read about right here.

These more advanced skills will be addressed in another guide available at some point in the future (if it isn't already) on triathlontaren.com OR you can always check out the Triathlon Taren YouTube channel and search for terms like "Triathlon Taren sighting", "Triathlon Taren catch", or anything else you've got swim questions about.

SWIM GEAR AND EQUIPMENT

As you start going to the pool more often, you're going to notice swimmers who have their own swim bags filled with different kinds of pool toys. At this point, we don't need to set you up with every last pool toy; as a developing triathlete, you have enough expenses so we'll get you started with just the essentials.

One of the nicest things about swimming is that the gear required is inexpensive. While you can easily spend $5,000 to get set up with your first triathlon bike, pool toys (even if you max out your pool bag) might only cost a grand total of about $200.

The gear we've recommended below is selected specifically for the unique requirements of an age-group triathlete. You're going to see different variations of all these items at the pool but you should be aware that a lot of people buy pool toys without an understanding of the unique benefits and drawbacks of each specific variation of a swim training device. Just because your friend uses a certain kind of flipper, or the fast lady in the pool swims with a certain kind of paddle, doesn't mean it's a useful tool for most age-group triathletes.

The entire list of the exact swim gear I use and recommend can be found here, on my Kit.com/triathlontaren page. If you're on Team Trainiac, all of our recommended swim gear is offered at as much as a 30 percent discount through one our Team Trainiac partners.

FINS/FLIPPERS

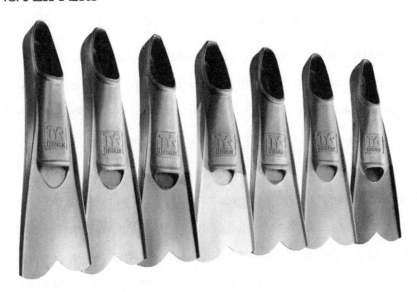

As you probably noticed throughout the drill progression, I often recommend fins or flippers. They allow triathletes to properly execute a drill by taking sinking legs out of the equation. That allows the athlete to develop the proper kick rate and will help with recovery by lengthening the body and smoothing out some of the knots and niggles that build up from cycling and running.

Unfortunately, swim fins are the pool "toy" triathletes most often select incorrectly. Short fins are typically too advanced for triathletes because they are actually designed for elite swimmers who already have a really good kick and want to strengthen it. Conversely, long fins are made for scuba divers and will slow down your kick rate.

What you're looking for in a fin is something that's about three to five inches longer than the end of your toes and somewhat pliable but with a rigid side. This type of fin is going to be long enough to create some nice fluidity in your kick, but it's not so long that it will slow down your kick. It's just the right length and just the right stiffness.

The fin I like to recommend is the TYR CrossBlade because it satisfies all the requirements for a triathlon swimmer and it's only about US$20 to US$30.

SNORKEL

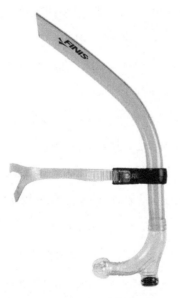

Much like the fins, a snorkel allows triathletes to focus on executing drills properly. Fortunately, there are far fewer options with swim snorkels, so it's easy to select one that'll work for you.

There's really only one requirement when it comes to snorkel selection, and that is to get a swim snorkel that goes up the center of your face, not along the side like a swim snorkel you'd use on vacation. The snorkels that go along the side of your face (including something as advanced and highly marketed to triathletes as the AMEO POWERBREATHER), don't allow your chin to rest on your shoulder, which is one of the key touch points that we have to focus on during a lot of our drills and regular swimming.

There are a couple of features you might want to include or avoid for bonus points. Some snorkels will have a clean-out valve that allows a buildup of water and saliva to collect in an area away from your mouth so you don't choke. Advanced swimmers won't benefit much from this, but new swimmers will appreciate not getting a mouthful of liquid every few breaths. Finally, you'll see on my Kit.com/triathlontaren page, I recommend a FINIS snorkel; oddly enough, you don't want the FINIS Freestyle Snorkel even though we triathletes swim freestyle. This snorkel has a really severe bend and I hear a lot of feedback from triathletes saying it bends so much that it actually bends back into the water. Instead, I recommend the FINIS Swimmer's Snorkel because it is inexpensive, it has a clean-out valve, and it has just the right amount of bend. Final note: If you're looking at the FINIS Swimmer's Snorkel, try to get the older model which has the clean-out valve, not the newer model with the molded headrest. In my testing of the newer model, it's less customizable so it might not fit for everyone.

PULL BUOY

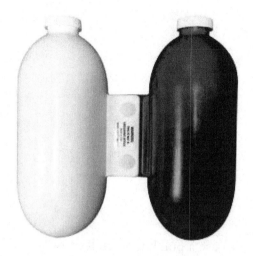

You may have noticed we didn't include any drills that use a pull buoy in this system. As soon as you develop these foundational swim skills and move on to doing full swim workouts again, a pull buoy will be the next-most critical tool you use.

Really, any pull buoy will work just fine, but if you want the best pull buoy on the market for only about $12 more than most other pull buoys, splurge and get the Eney Buoy. The Eney Buoy is made with two chambers of air that look kind of like a one-liter, plastic pop bottle. Because the Eney Buoy is plastic, it doesn't get moldy like foam pull buoys, and the chambers can each be filled up with water, making this a multifunctional tool that can add buoyancy or drag (which are used in some of the more advanced swim sets we use on Team Trainiac.)

ANKLE STRAP

If you're going to use a pull buoy, you'll want to get an ankle strap. Using a pull buoy by itself creates buoyancy at the hips and gives triathletes a false sense that they're swimming correctly; when a pull buoy is used by itself, it folds a swimmer's body in half, creating a pivot point in the body. That pivot point undoes any work the athlete has done to create a nice long, singular, float-like-a-log body position.

Pull-buoy work on Team Trainiac is always paired with an ankle strap and quite often a snorkel, so the body line is treated as one long unit and you don't create new, bad technique.

The most common ankle strap you'll see is an old bike-tire tube that's tied up, or if swimmers really splurge, they might get something resembling a very thick rubber band. However, these two types of ankle straps often become loose and allow an athlete to kick a little bit, which we want to avoid. Instead, I recommend the TYR Rally Training Strap. If you can find Speedo Ankle Locks, those are even better but they're out of production and tough to find.

MIRRORED GOGGLES

To keep your number of equipment purchases to a minimum, I'm going to recommend a pair of goggles that will work both in the pool and in open water. The FINIS circuit mirrored goggles are inexpensive enough that you can use them in the pool without worrying too much about the chlorine damaging them. The mirrored finish on these goggles will take glare off the water during your race and allow you to see much better. (Actually, any mirrored goggle will work fine for open-water swimming, but some might be too dark to use in the pool.)

One final note about goggles: Triathletes who find that goggles leak often have purchased the biggest goggles with a huge silicone gasket. In my experience, this makes it harder to get a good seal with the silicone gasket because there's so much more material that has to suction onto your face. In order to make these big goggles fit properly, they need to be tightened down a lot. On average, I find the best goggles are smaller and fit comfortably without much pressure.

CHAPTER 6

SWIMMING FORWARD

HOW SOON WILL YOU GET FASTER?

Quite often when I work with developing triathletes, I prescribe some mix of these drills to them. They'll try them for one workout, or maybe for a few minutes at the start of every workout, but then they go back to regular swimming because they feel if they're not swimming, they're not making progress.

During his teens, an elite youth triathlete friend of mine was stuck around 5:30 for a 400-meter time trial. He was already a very good swimmer but he needed to get under 5:00 to make the front swim pack in the races he was competing in. He took six weeks away from the swim squad and just worked on technique. When he came back to the swim squad, there were a few weeks of re-familiarizing himself with his speed but soon enough, he was swimming under 5:00 per 400 meters.

If such a huge improvement can be made by an athlete who already had an amazing technique, think about how much improvement you can make in your speed by simply improving your technique!

You can and will improve if you stay focused and patient. The difficult part of the task ahead is that it's going to feel like you're stepping backward, spending time splashing around, doing "kids' drills" in the shallow end.

Now, you might find that even after going through all these drills and developing total comfort and body awareness, when you come back to regular swimming, your times are actually slower (and I can guarantee you're not going to see the rapid improvements in 400-meter times that my friend did). I've personally gone through this mind-bender of a one-step-backward, two-steps-forward process twice.

Most recently, over the winter of 2018–19, I was swimming four times a week with a lot of focus on technique and improving my kick to get my body line more streamlined. A typical workout had 40–60 percent of the workout focused on very intentional, sequential drills. I showed up every day, didn't cut corners, and noticed my ability to execute the drills was getting better and better. But when I'd swim a normal 100 or 200, it would be slower than during the previous race season.

Toward the end of the winter, I went down to Los Angeles to work on my swim with Gerry Rodrigues from Tower 26 and when I got out of the pool after the very first swim, he said, "You're a completely different swimmer than the last time you were here a year ago. You're starting to look like the pros who weren't swimmers but turned themselves into swimmers." Here I was thinking I was making zero progress, yet he was pumped. I told him it didn't feel like I was getting any faster. Gerry has a habit of putting things "elegantly bluntly," and he said, "I don't know what you're expecting. You've been doing nothing but technique all winter. Talk to me in a few months, after we've incorporated more normal swimming to prep for the race season."

I still wasn't very confident that I'd made much progress, but Gerry's system has worked for a ton of athletes over the years so I figured I'd wait and see what happened. Well, over the next two months as we transitioned away from winter technique-focused swimming to more steady swimming, my speed increased by leaps and bounds. Within just a matter of a few weeks of doing 100s and 200s again, my times were faster than anything I could even touch the previous season. And I could hold this speed effortlessly for hundreds and hundreds of meters! YouTube search "Triathlon Taren Results from 1 Year of Dedicated Swim Training" and you'll see the one-step-backward, two-steps-forward process that swim progress takes.

Eventually, when I raced a couple months after seeing Gerry (and was still slightly unsure of what my 2019 swimming would look like) I raced my first event of the season and not only did I have the best race swim I've ever had, I was fresh enough to get out of that swim and put out a personal best on the bike of 2:18 for 90k. That clocked in as the sixth-best bike split in the field.

So, to relate this back to you, even if the swim pace clock on the wall says you're no faster in the short term, if you can breathe easier, if you're getting your legs up closer to the surface of the water, and if you've got better body awareness and don't feel yourself wiggling side to side as much, then YOU ARE MAKING SWIM PROGRESS! As such, your times will eventually get faster—there's virtually no way they can't.

If you're diligent, consistent, and honest with yourself about totally focusing on following this system, I guarantee you'll see results.

Now, if you should find that you get stuck on a drill and just can't seem to reach the point where I've indicated that you've mastered the drill, it may be that you're doing something incorrectly with the drill. Remember, these drills may sound simple in this book but it's the nuances that make or break your swim progression. Because triathletes typically don't have great body awareness in the water, it will be hard to perform the drills correctly if you don't know what to focus on. Watch and rewatch the videos at triathlontaren.com/swimfoundations often.

MOVING FORWARD

Here's what I challenge you to do. This is going to be one of the most important things you do from this entire book. Just this short exercise alone will result in more improvement than anything else you've read about thus far.

Pull out whatever you take notes in. Whether it's a note-taking app on your phone or a scrap piece of paper, it doesn't matter, just get it out. In that document, write down the first three words you associate with swimming.

Here's the harder part. Go swim a 100-meter or yard time trial as fast as you possibly can. Also swim a 1,000-yard or meter time trial as fast as you possibly can without stopping. (Or if you need to stop, mark down how far you made it.) Write those times (or the distance you made it to in the 1,000 if you had to take a break) in the same place you wrote the three words you associate with swimming.

Now the work comes. Go through the swim system you've read about in this book. Do it diligently, don't cut corners, be patient, and be confident that you're doing the right things.

Then (and this is where it gets fun), one month after you've completed the swim drill system from this book and have started returning to performing regular swim workouts, do another 100- and 1000-yard or meter swim, tracking your time again. Also, write down the first three words that come to your mind again. Then compare the times AND the three words to what you wrote on the very first day. The progress you will have made in a few short months will astound you—but only if you follow this system as prescribed, without shortcuts or modifications.

Thank you so much for letting me be a part of your triathlon journey and I can't wait for the day you write to tell me how comfortable you've become in the water thanks to this simple system of easy drills.

Later, Trainiacs!

GLOSSARY

Channel: As I use "arm channel" in this book, it refers to the chute alongside the body from the edge of the head to the outside edge of the shoulder. This channel is where the hand should enter the water—and stay roughly within—all the way back through the stroke.

Rep: A repetition of a movement. If you perform 10 push-ups, you've performed 10 "reps".

Set: A set is a group of repetitions. If you perform 10 push-ups, three times, for a total of 30 push-ups, you've performed "three sets of 10 reps".

Pull Buoy: A floating device that can be put between the thighs while swimming to facilitate specific drills.

Drag: In the water, drag is what will slow a swimmer down while moving forward through the water. We want to reduce drag by minimizing the frontal area of a swimmer.

Sighting: Looking up and out of the water to see where you're going while swimming.

Body Line: Refers to the body's position in relation to the water. We want a body line with the back of the head, the butt, and the heels at the surface of the water. We also want a body line that swims straight in the water without the legs swaying side to side.

Ankle Band/Strap: A swim training device that allows swimmers to strap their ankles together for specific drills.

TheraBand: Long lengths of stretchy rubber bands that look like flat sheets, about 5" wide, that can be used for specific exercises.

StretchCordz: Long lengths of stretchy rubber bands that look like cables. We use these to strengthen our stability in swimming.

Buoys: Large floating devices that sit in the water to mark a swim course.

Masters Swimming: An organized adult swim group that typically meets at regular times and usually is led by a coach.

ACKNOWLEDGEMENTS

The content of this book, and my personal swim progression, would not have been possible without the contributions of three excellent coaches.

Matt Dixon, head coach and founder of Purple Patch Fitness, has an elite swimming background and an approach to triathlon training that I greatly respect and try to emulate with the athletes I coach. I've worked with Matt in various capacities on his Purple Patch marketing, and even taken part in a Purple Patch training camp. Watching Matt approach endurance training was tremendously valuable.

Brenton Ford, founder of Effortless Swimming, is one of the most talented swim stroke analyzers I've ever seen. He has a great ability to not just identify swim faults and areas of improvement but assign the exact drill, sequence, swim thought, or workout swimmers should use to improve their swim stroke.

I owe a massive thanks to Gerry Rodrigues, head coach of Tower 26. Not only has Gerry been my swim coach, but he's been a good friend and mentor as I've entered the triathlon industry. A great deal of what's found in this book is borne from the lessons Gerry has taught me through his podcast, his Tower 26 coaching platform (which I highly recommend), and the time I've spent working with him one-on-one in Los Angeles. Without Gerry's guidance, I wouldn't be where I am in swimming or the triathlon world. Thank you!

And finally, to my wife Kim, thank you for being okay with me parading around in front of a worldwide audience in a Speedo. I couldn't do any of this without you!

NEXT STEPS

Now that you're done with this book, here are some next steps for you.

1. JOIN THE TRAINIAC COMMUNITY

There are so many ways to join the Trainiac community! Here's how:

Visit us online at <u>triathlontaren.com</u> for free resources, valuable training info, and more.

Visit <u>teamtrainiac.com</u> to get signed up to the most accessible triathlon training platform in the world. For a fraction of the price of a one-on-one coach, get a fully customizable, year-round training plan to get you prepared for your races, no matter your level of experience!

Visit **protriathlontraining.com** to take your triathlon game to the next level with training advice, tips and tricks from some of the top professional triathletes and coaches in the world. Easy-to-follow modules will help you make game-changing tweaks and improvements to the way you race.

2. FOLLOW US ON SOCIAL MEDIA

For tips, tricks, training updates and more, follow us on our most active social media channels:

YOUTUBE: youtube.com/triathlontaren

INSTAGRAM: @triathlontaren

FACEBOOK: facebook.com/triathlontaren

3. SUBSCRIBE TO THE TRIATHLON TAREN PODCAST

The top-rated Triathlon podcast in the world on iTunes, the Triathlon Taren podcast brings you interviews with the who's-who in triathlon including professional triathletes, inspiring age-groupers and more! Download the podcast wherever you get your favourite podcasts.

4. SHARE THIS BOOK

Please write us a review on Amazon and let your fellow triathletes know about us! Spreading the word helps to reach new readers, to grow the Trainiac community, and it allows us to bring you more great resources.

You can write an Amazon review right on the Amazon page for this book. It really helps us a lot.

THANK YOU! And we'll see ya soon, Trainiac!

ABOUT THE AUTHOR

"Triathlon Taren" Gesell is a triathlete who has become known for his wildly popular Triathlon Taren YouTube page, Instagram account and podcast, where he shares tips, tricks, hacks and time-tested knowledge to help age-groupers get to their start lines confident and their finish lines strong. Based in Winnipeg, Canada, Triathlon Taren is also the head coach of Team Trainiac, a training platform supporting a growing community of triathletes from all around the world.

Made in the USA
Middletown, DE
07 March 2020